A Year Without a Man

A Year Without a Man

A Year Without a Man

A Transformational Journey

Barbara DeHart and Gayle Long, LMFT

A YEAR WITHOUT, LLC
NEVADA CITY, CALIFORNIA, USA

A Year Without, LLC
Nevada City, CA

Library of Congress Control Number: 2024906747
Paperback ISBN: 979-8-9898937-0-6
eBook ISBN: 979-8-9898937-1-3

Book cover and interior design by Christina Thiele
Editorial production by KN Literary Arts

www.ayearwithoutaman.com

This book is dedicated to all those who fear being alone and believe that they can't let go of one relationship until they have another to hold on to.

Contents

1

Prologue

I am on the floor. I can feel the wood grain against my face. I can hear Gayle's voice in the distance.

"Barb, are you okay?"

I try to respond but can't speak. I hear her as she instructs my daughter, Sammy, in a calm but firm manner, "Everything is going to be all right, but I need you to call 9-1-1." She repeats, "Sammy, call 9-1-1."

At that, I try to stir, but my body is not responding. I don't understand what is happening. Gayle and I were having coffee on the deck. I came inside to use the bathroom. Now, I am here. On the floor. In the hall.

"Come on, Barb. Wake up," Gayle pleads.

"I am awake. I'm fine," I try to say, but my words aren't coming out. I try again. "I am fine," I think I say. Again, no sound.

And then I slip back into darkness.

THE ROLLER COASTER YEARS

Owning our story can be hard, but not nearly as difficult as spending our lives running from it.

—Brené Brown

On the outside, we were very different women. Gayle was a stay-at-home wife and mom with a gorgeous custom home, three children, and plenty of time to shop and volunteer. She loved fashion, décor, and putting together an impeccable appearance from the wisp on her bangs to the point of her shoes. Barb was a technology executive with a get-things-done approach to life. She had two children and multiple properties and investments. She opted for perfectly pressed slacks and a button-up blouse for work but was comfortable doing Saturday chores with no makeup and a baseball cap. We'd met years before, but our fateful reacquaintance on a Halloween night revealed we had a lot in common—including two very big secrets and a desire to stop the chaos in our lives. Our connection and shared obsessions put us on a course toward a radical idea: to live a year without a man.

2

Halloween, Six Months Earlier

Barb

I look in my bedroom mirror at my matching camo jacket, trousers, and cap and sigh. *This is the beauty of Halloween*, the soldier within me says to my reflection. We can pretend to be whatever we want. There is no bravery emanating from my weary frame.

On the outside, I am the picture of independence. I am a senior-level executive at a tech company, known for getting things done. I am financially secure; in fact, I'm the one who buys businesses and investment properties, not my husband. On the outside, people see a woman who raises her children in a loving environment and who manages a career that includes world travel while still maintaining a rich, full home life. I'm seemingly "perfect, whole, and complete," as I like to say.

Only those closest to me know the truth. I have spent my entire adult life seeking that perfect, whole, and complete Barb. I have spent countless hours and more money than I care to admit on self-improvement. I've seen all the therapists: psychotherapists, hypnotherapists, marriage and family thera-pists, trauma therapists. I've seen psychics, bodyworkers, and healers of all kinds. I've worked twelve-step programs, read a library of self-help books, and gone to countless workshops.

You name it; I've tried it. But, in this moment, despite all that work, I have to admit—with one relationship ending and another complicated one beginning—the cold, hard truth: I do not know how to live in this world without a man.

Despite all the self-help and therapy, I spent the majority of my adult life trying to find happiness through relationships with men (lots of men). The if/then tape was loud in my mind: *If I find the right man, then I will finally be happy.*

Something inside compelled me to avoid being alone, and I spent nearly every day of my adult life in a relationship with a man. If I wasn't in a committed relationship, I was dating someone. And pity the boyfriend or husband who tried to play the role of partner or lover, because there was no way he was ever going to win, no way he could ever be good enough, could love me enough, or make me feel secure enough for me to be able to ever really let his love in. And every time, no matter what, I'd be the one to leave first in order to avoid the risk of him rejecting me.

As I leave for the Halloween party, I realize all these habits and patterns are tucked into my army fatigues. I'm feeling a little bit like a fraud and realizing the image of the perfect soldier couldn't be more different than the reality of my life. It's a mess. "Let's do this," I say to my nervous reflection in the mirror.

Although we had separated more than a year before, my husband, Steve, and I had maintained our family rituals—until this year. Historically, we would have attended this party as a family. But this year Sammy and I were going alone.

"Come on, Sammy," I yell to my eleven-year-old daughter who is struggling to tuck her long blond hair into the hood of her purple octopus hat. I grab our contribution to the potluck, a soy noodle salad prepared fresh by our local deli. Together, the Soldier and the Octopus head out into the night air of our charming little town in the foothills of Northern California, the streets already teeming with little goblins as we walk a few blocks down the hill to the party.

I feel nervous as we enter the home of our long-time friends. As comfortable as I am with the separation, I feel anxious as I walk into the party without my husband. I'm worried that people will ask me, "Where's Steve?" and I'll be faced with a decision: Do I lie and say he couldn't make it, or do I tell the truth that we are separated and have been for a while?

As I suspected, "Where is Steve?" is the question attached to each hello. Separation does that; eventually, all our couple events become singles events. Where we used to attend together, now I attend alone. I am really good at projecting my inner fears onto others and worry that our couple friends, most of whom have been married to each other forever, will think less of me for leaving my husband. I feel a bit more sadness each time someone asks about him.

A warm feeling of relief rushes over me as I run into Gayle, a long-ago friend whom I haven't seen in many years. Always one to make a big statement, she is well put together in her Superwoman costume with thigh-high, shiny, red boots and red cape, her hair and makeup perfectly done. She is sporting a huge, friendly smile. The sexy confidence of her costume contrasts with the practicality and blandness of my military uniform. Both alter egos seem fitting. After all, I feel like I'm fighting a war, and Gayle has always had life figured out.

Gayle grew up in a traditional, upper-middle-class family in Marin County, California. Her professional father left every morning at 7 a.m. and returned to a family dinner at 6:35 p.m. Her stay-at-home mother, who left her nursing career when Gayle was born, dedicated herself to maintaining the home and raising her children. It seemed only natural that Gayle would marry well, and when she married a psychiatrist, she became the consummate doctor's wife. She was the stay-at-home mom who raised her perfect family (two girls and a boy) while her husband provided for the family. She fits seamlessly into the upper-class neighborhood where they built their custom-made, luxury home. She's curvy and fit, stylish and sensuous. Even a trip to the grocery store is a reason to put her makeup and hair perfectly in place. Her appearance draws the notice of anyone in the room, and she knows how to use that to her advantage.

Standing between the kitchen and the dining room at this Halloween party, Gayle asks, "How are you?"

And, although I hate conditioned responses, I have become quite good at employing them. "I'm fine," I say with a smile, "How are you?"

Gayle looks directly into my eyes, reaches out, and touches my arm. And, with her best therapist voice, she says, "No, really, how are you?"

Suddenly, time stops. I realize that in all the time that Steve and I have been separated, no one has ever genuinely asked me that question—not like this, anyway. She really wants to know how I am.

I can feel tears welling up in my eyes. All I can say is, "Honestly, being here without Steve is really hard. This is all new. I feel lost. But look at you, Superwoman."

Gayle just smiles. "Do you want the truth?" she asks.

"Of course!"

"The truth. . . ." Gayle hesitates. "The truth is that an hour ago, I was standing in front of the mirror in my bathroom taking off my wedding ring for the first time, wondering if anyone would notice. Superwoman is pretty far from how I'm really feeling right now. Greg and I are getting a divorce, and I just started grad school to become a therapist and start my own career. I think, if anything, I have lost my superpowers!" She laughs.

"Wow, what?" I ask, concerned. "I had no idea you two had gotten to that point."

Focusing her attention back on me, Gayle asks, "What happened with you and Steve? I remember your wedding— you guys seemed so happy."

"I finally realized I couldn't fix him. I feel like I spent years trying to get him to find his 'happy place.' At first, I thought it was me, then I thought it was his career, but ultimately, nothing seemed to make him happy. Then, one day I realized that nothing I could do or provide would ever be enough. He had to find that for himself. He was just unhappy, and I couldn't change that. So, I decided to stop trying."

"Hmmm, wait, what . . . what about therapy?" Gayle asks.

"Well, he was willing to try therapy and anything else I suggested, but he would only do it for me. I needed him to want to become happier and healthier for himself, not for me. And the bottom line was that he just wasn't, nor was he present for our relationship or me. My drive for success was mis-matched with his desire to live a simple, less driven life. I kept trying to change the external circumstances; nothing worked.

"Then one day, after I continued to push him to go deeper, to find a way to feel happy about his life, to engage more intimately with me, he said that was all he had to offer. As hard as it was to hear it, I appreciated the truth. When I finally got it, I knew it was time to look for an exit. So, I bought a small house here in town, and Sammy and I moved from the ranch out in the country. Our split has been amicable, so even though we live apart, we still operate very much as a family. We are so good at it that some of our friends still don't know we're separated, which is what makes tonight so difficult. Obviously, that's the *Reader's Digest* version.

"What happened with you guys? I can't believe you and Greg are splitting up. You two have been together forever too."

"Yeah, over twenty-two years," Gayle says, sadly.

"I had no idea. What happened?"

Gayle sighs. "It's been a long time coming . . . too much to go into right now, but, we've finally decided to end it. We're still in our house. The kids don't even know yet, but the truth is, it's over."

We move from the kitchen to the back steps where we sit huddled together, another friend stepping over us on her way inside. "You guys okay?" she asks. In unison, we respond, "We're fine." We laugh.

After our friend is out of earshot, Gayle turns to me and says, "You know what 'fine' really stands for, right? Fucked-up, Insecure, Neurotic, and Emotional." We both laugh out loud.

In this moment, Gayle's warmth and understanding make me feel comfortable and safe. We continue to talk about things that really matter—the changes going on in our lives and the struggles associated with them. We're both navigating similarly difficult waters, so we make plans to meet for dinner the next day.

And for the rest of the evening, the answer to "Where's Steve?" becomes a simple, "He couldn't make it."

3

Our First Dinner

Barb

I park in the heart of our historic gold rush town and walk past the Victorian facades of quaint shops and locally owned restaurants. I open the door to Lefty's Grill, known for fresh California cuisine, and see Gayle sitting in a booth by the large street-side windows.

"Sorry I'm late," I say as I settle into the booth. The truth is I am always just a little bit late. It's my way to ensure I won't be alone. Even a few minutes of waiting for others to join me at a restaurant leaves me feeling unsettled and insecure."

"It's fine. I just got here myself," Gayle says. "I'm always a little late too," she confesses with an understanding smile. Another trait we seem to have in common. "It's so great to reconnect with you. It's been a crazy time."

We order dinner, deciding to split a Caesar salad and glazed salmon sitting on a bed of butternut squash and basmati rice, paired with a nice Sauvignon Blanc. We don't know it yet, but this will become our standard order for many weekly dinners to come. We clink our glasses together. "To reconnecting," Gayle says.

"So fill me in. What exactly happened with you and Greg?"

Gayle takes a deep breath in and lets it out. "Where do I start? You know that nagging feeling that something is wrong, but you just can't quite put your finger on what it is? I had that with Greg for a long time. I kept ignoring it and blaming it on anything and everything other than what it really was. Then, about five years ago as I was about to step into the shower, I noticed he had forgotten his cellphone behind that morning when he had left to go fishing. Just then, it pinged with a text message from a woman he worked with. It was a Sunday morning, and my first thought was, *That's strange, why is she texting him now?* I looked at the text, realized there were many texts from her, and without one ounce of guilt, I dove in. What happened next was one of those knee-buckling-room-spinning-ears-ringing-nauseous-I-think-I'm-going-to-puke-I-can't-stand-because-my-legs-don't-work experiences. I went into shock, realizing I had discovered my worst fear. Greg was cheating on me."

"Oh my God," I say. "What?"

"I just stared at his phone. I mean, I couldn't believe it. There were so many messages. And they were all so intimate. I fell to the floor and read them. All of them. They were playful, explicitly sexual, and went back many months. They referred to one another as 'boyfriend' and 'girlfriend.' My husband. And this woman."

"Holy shit. That's awful," I say. "Are you serious? Oh my God, are you okay?"

"I know! It was literally my worst nightmare coming true. After that, I thought I was going to be sick. I could feel the blood draining from my head. You know, even though I had suspected he was interested in other women, I really didn't believe deep down that he would ever actually cross that line. Despite all we'd been through in nearly two decades of marriage, I still saw him as my soul mate, my faithful husband who would never cheat on me. Realizing that he was having an affair changed how I saw everything about our marriage and our relationship."

"Gayle, I am so sorry," I say.

"Yeah, I was a total mess. After falling to my knees in the bathroom, I crawled to the phone and called a girlfriend I'd met at Al-Anon for help. She agreed to come over. When she found me, I still had his cellphone in my hand and was lying naked on the bathroom floor while frantically writing down all of the excruciatingly painful details I'd found in the text messages. She draped a robe over me because I hadn't even realized I was still naked. I was in a deeply dissociated state of shock. She turned off the shower and let me cry. It still seems surreal when I talk about it now. It's like I've detached from the memory. It was one of those moments after which nothing would ever be the same again."

"Wow. . . ." I say. "Well, at least you knew the truth, I guess."

"Yeah, I know. I had begun to convince myself that my intuition, that inner voice inside me, was just exaggerating. But deep down, I knew what was happening. I remember, for years, getting this buzzing feeling in the pit of my stomach every night at the sound of the garage door opening because I never knew what kind of mood or state of mind he would be in when he got home. After finding the texts, I knew I wasn't crazy. I had my proof! I finally had all the evidence and had cracked the case."

"Wait, I'm confused. That was five years ago? You're just splitting up now?"

"I know it sounds crazy. Looking back, I can see that finding those messages was a wake-up call that I didn't fully get. I knew that our relationship was a far cry from what I thought it would be when we first got married. But I wanted to believe we could still make it work." Gayle sighs sadly. "I felt a huge chunk of my heart break off and die that day, and I kind of just stayed numb from that trauma for years while at the same time dragging him into marriage counseling, a couples Bible study group, and even the Landmark Forum. None of it worked. He stuck to his story that he wasn't cheating."

"But you had the proof. It was on the phone. They called each other boyfriend and girlfriend."

"He claimed it didn't mean anything. He said that was just how they jokingly referred to each other. Even though I had the proof, he denied it. I never got a sincere apology or any movement toward the loving connection I craved."

"But you stayed! I can't imagine staying in a relationship like that. I don't think I could have lived that lie," I say, taking a sip of my wine.

"Yeah. . . . I just couldn't imagine having to support myself. I really didn't see myself as anything other than a wife and mother, and I never wanted to break up our family. In a weird way, it actually helped me stay because at least then I knew the truth. I knew I wasn't crazy. My suspicions were not unfounded. It turns out he had a number of vices that could all be deemed mistresses of one sort or another: alcohol, drugs, golf, and other women. They were his priority. They all took him away from me. They had his time, attention, and affection, and I simply pretended they didn't exist. I always wanted to be a priority but never was. There was no 'we' in our relationship.

"I had started therapy years before to cope with some of his vices, and in one of my weekly therapy sessions, after finding out about Greg's affair, I stubbornly said with resolve, 'I accept that this is my life and that divorce is not an option.' I truly believed that at the time. I also believed I could never possibly live alone. The thought of being alone petrified me."

"So, it was easier for you to go into denial and stay? I completely understand how the thought of breaking up your family must have been very scary for you."

"Yes. Denial and avoidance became our mutual companions. And we just went on with our lives, going through the motions. One day turned into the next, then months turned into years—that kind of thing. I've been operating pretty much on autopilot ever since."

"So what made you finally decide to split?"

"Well, to be honest"—Gayle's face lit up as she spoke—"it was an invitation to go skydiving."

Gayle

My belief that I needed to stay married forever probably would have prevailed had I not (quite uncharacteristically) gone skydiving one day. Although I'm one to take risks and break the rules, hurling myself out of a perfectly good airplane 13,500 feet above ground is the single most terrifying thing I have ever done.

My girlfriends and I had decided to celebrate a friend's fiftieth birthday with this wild excursion. We paid extra money to ensure we could jump from the highest altitude possible without having to wear oxygen masks. I had to be weighed in order to figure out which guide to be paired with. I'm not sure what terrified me most, the number on the scale or the anticipation of jumping out of a plane. I was shocked when I saw the number on the scale beneath my feet. Until that moment, I hadn't realized how much I had given up and let my appearance and weight go.

I stood outside the plane, trembling with terror. I asked our guides so many questions that our jump was delayed by twenty minutes. "What happens if the chute doesn't open? When was the last time the backup sensor was tested? How old are the parachutes? How many people have died from jumping this past year? How many jumps have you done?"

"Over eight thousand," my guide answered.

My inner fear responded. *YOU ARE GOING TO DIE! Not only are you going to die, but you are going to die weighing more than 172 pounds, and you're going to die miserable!*

I did not want to put on that jumpsuit, partly out of a white-hot panicky buzz vibrating throughout my body and partly because the ninety-degree weather wasn't helping the sweat already dripping down my chest. But I wanted to stay strong in front of my girlfriends who were likely having similar internal battles. Besides, this was a "once-in-a-lifetime experi-ence" and something I had always wanted to do. So . . . now was the time.

Greg had left for work that morning without even saying goodbye. Although we were still speaking and going through the motions of staying married and being a family, by this time, he had been sleeping downstairs in the guest quarters for months. As he left silently, I thought to myself, *Does he not realize that this could be the last time he ever sees me? Or does he just not care?*

Back in the drop zone, I could delay the inevitable no longer. We were paired with the guides and then they marched us, single file, in the hot summer air, up the ramp to the open twin-engine airplane. Inside, strapped to our guides, we straddled one of the two benches. Twelve jumpers were on board. Glancing over at my friend Mimi, I noticed she was white as a ghost. I could hear my own heart beating in my ears. My mouth was very dry. As the skydiving company captured everything on film, I tried to smile for the camera. I wanted to go first to get it over with. As the plane rattled upward, my thoughts ran toward my three kids and how they would react when they received the news that their mom had been killed in a skydiving accident.

When we got to 13,500 feet, I looked up and watched two experienced jumpers vanish through the hole in the plane where the door was. I was up next.

I can do this! I shouted to myself inside. *It's been a good life. And now I'm saying goodbye to it. One, two, three. . . .* And I fell backward into the open air. The only sound I could hear was the wind rushing past my head. I had to tilt my chin down because the air pressure surging up my nose was painful. I had one minute to freefall before it would be time to pull the chute. To my surprise, I didn't feel any sensation of falling; rather, I felt suspended in midair. I was FREE! Truly free. No fear, no worry, pure surrender, disembodied. With my eye on the wrist altimeter, I reached back with my right hand for the handle that was supposed to open the chute and pulled hard.

Whoosh! The chute opened and jerked violently back on the straps that ran across my triple-D breasts, which protested in pain and reminded me of the fact that I still had a body.

Then I felt myself gliding in pure silence. Nirvana, peace, serenity. . . . I had admittedly experimented with some drugs in the past and can honestly say that I had never been so high. Yet I was in control now. Pulling to the right, I flew to the right. Pulling to the left, I soared left. It was like being in those dreams where you are flying and all is well. Time no longer existed.

Until it did.

Suddenly, the stone-cold reality of the rock-hard earth was approaching rapidly. I wanted to stay here, high above the ground, way up in the air. I wanted to stay in this free space, this neutral zone between the trapezes, forever. Then I realized I had one choice: to trust. To trust that all would be well, that my guide knew what he was doing, and that together, we would meet the ground softly.

It was not.

He did not.

We did not.

The grey-pebbled landing strip that we were supposed to have landed on safely was behind us before I knew it. My knees were bent to my chest as he had instructed me back in the training room when—BOOM!—we hit the ground *hard*. He had assured me that his feet would hit the ground first, but they didn't. Instead, my butt hit the ground first, and I found myself watching the cracked ground, covered in spiky thistle plants, whizzing by. Then, quite suddenly, we stopped on the ground. No movement. I froze.

I heard other people shouting for me to get up, but I knew

that would be painful, so I said, "No, I'm good; I'll just stay sitting here."

Apparently, I was in shock because I hadn't yet felt any pain, nor had I realized that the other jumpers were going to land behind me and that I was in their way. My guide and another young tatted-up guide lifted me up, and I walked awkwardly off the field. When we got inside, they told me that we had missed the landing strip (clearly!), and I told them that something was definitely wrong at the base of my spine.

The next day, my chiropractor informed me that my tailbone was dislocated, which, I found out moments later, requires Vaseline and expert fingers inserted into one's rectum to correct. She yanked my spine back into its proper position, and I felt intense relief.

As uncomfortable and scary as that tailbone adjustment felt physically, it was nothing compared to the enormous leap I had just taken emotionally. There, in my doctor's office, I realized that as I had limped gracelessly off that airfield the day before, I had walked directly into a new life, leaving my fear behind. My fear of dying, and perhaps more importantly, my fear of living. Floating in silence above the Earth, I had been shot into communion with a life force energy that I had suppressed for decades. I had been living on autopilot, resigned to being a submissive wife in what had become a loveless marriage where I let Greg have all the control. My fear of being alone had kept me in my marriage. Now, I felt alive and in control of my destiny.

Skydiving shocked the impossibilities right out of my brain. The irony was that while on the plane, my anxiety and nervousness were at their height, but the freedom came as soon as I jumped. If I could face that fear and survive, I could do anything. And just like that, I became fearless for a while, and I began to plan.

Barb

I thought Gayle was incredibly brave to go skydiving—and what a revelation she had. But she'd never been on her own. Although she had held jobs and volunteer positions over the years (real estate, managing Greg's psychiatry practice, mediator, counselor), Greg supported her and their family. How would she manage?

"I realized I would need a way to support myself," Gayle tells me, "so I applied to grad school. I'm a full-time student now. And once I'm through with my 3,000 clinical hours, I'll be a licensed psychotherapist in California."

"That's a lot to manage, but it sounds like you have it figured out, right? After so many years of being completely dependent on Greg, what an accomplishment."

"Well, going back to school was just the beginning," Gayle says, then hesitates. She looks down at her plate for a long time and continues. "Shortly after that day, breaking all my rules, I also finally returned the call from a man who had been asking me out to lunch for several months and said yes. We've been seeing each other for a while, and now he's all I think about. I see a future with him, and I'm not sure I would have the courage to leave if I didn't have him. We're planning to be together, but we want to do it the right way."

"The right way?" I ask. "What does that mean?"

Gayle pauses. Then, she gently leans in and confesses quietly: "He's married. As a matter of fact, that is how I refer to him: Mr. Married. He's in a miserable marriage and says it is the bane of his existence. We haven't had sex yet, but we are in love, and it just feels so good. Our plan is for both of us to get divorced, wait a year or so, and then be together. Like I said, we want to do this the 'right way.' We want to be above board."

"So, wait, you aren't having sex with him?" I ask suspiciously.

"Well, it's not that I don't want to be with him now. I really, really do, but he won't let that happen. Not yet anyway. The temptation is killing me, but there's excitement in the anticipation. I feel like I found a new leading man, a man who is healthy and secure and wants to be with me. Like I said, being without a man is not in my plans. So, I'm still trying to figure it all out, but I'm totally in love with this guy who's not really available, and I'm trying to get my shit together." Gayle laughs, a little cynically, and takes a long drink from her wine glass. "Man, it sure feels good to share that. I feel so relieved."

My mind is racing. *Oh my God. Oh my God. Me too. Me too,* I keep thinking. But all I can say is, "I also have someone in my life I am a bit fixated on."

Gayle and I, on the surface, were polar opposites: I had never learned to rely on a man, and Gayle had never learned not to. Yet neither of us had been without one. I couldn't bring myself to admit that not only were we in the same boat, but we were also in the same seat, careening down the same river, desperately seeking the same paddle.

4

The Misters

Gayle—Mr. Married

Sitting at a community event, I had my first encounter with Mr. Married. A real estate developer turned executive, he sits down at the same table. He's paying attention to me, really paying attention to me—and I notice his strong jawline, the high and tight haircut, his big blue eyes, and the deep calming voice. (Although I don't realize it now, he is a reflection of my dad.) I start telling him about attending the Landmark Forum, a transformative learning model that helps people with their relationships and life satisfaction. It had been one of those desperate attempts to save my marriage, and I'd forced Greg to go with me in hopes that he'd start making some changes. Mr. Married listens; he wants to know more. He hints that his marriage, too, is not happy. The magnetic pull is undeniable. The more we talk, the more my body buzzes.

When I leave that evening, I feel like I'm hovering above the ground. (I know now that oxytocin and dopamine were flooding my body.) He is so different from Greg—sharply dressed, exuding masculinity yet kind-hearted and warm, conservative, and outgoing—and he wanted to know about me.

We often run into each other at community events. But it takes months before I respond to his requests to meet for lunch. When I finally do, we spend half the time talking "business" about an upcoming fundraiser we both support and half the time talking about his messed-up relationships. It turns out that he is actually trying to break off an affair with another woman, but she's claimed that she wouldn't survive if he leaves her. No doubt I can help him with that.

He also dives into how bad his marriage is. *Oh really? You want to talk about miserable marriages? Say no more.* I'm hooked. We commiserate over our tense home life and loveless spouses. The relief and comfort of telling him how disappointed and dejected I am feeling at home is immense. As we leave, we hug—and my body buzzes with that same high I felt the first night I met him.

A few weeks later, Greg sees the texts on my phone about getting together with Mr. Married for lunch. He confronts me about it, suspicious if *I* am the one having an affair. Nothing has happened between Mr. Married and me (besides feeling a high any time I saw him). I do confess to Greg: "When I was having lunch with him, I found myself sharing stuff with him that I used to share with you. And I want that to be with you."

"I don't give a shit who you have lunch with," he replies. "You should probably tell him how crazy you are."

Of course, he doesn't care, I think. *Our life together is a charade.*

So I keep seeing Mr. Married, telling myself that we are not doing anything wrong. On one early date, we are hugging, and as we turn our heads, we kiss. It has been years since I've had a clean, luxurious kiss (Greg has a chewing tobacco habit). This seals the deal for me—I know we are meant to be together. But I'm not going to cross the line sexually even though every time I see him in a suit, I'm turned on. I'm going to remain "above board" with this relationship.

One night during an extremely rare chance to be on the phone together, he tells me his wife has just stormed out of the house. We profess what we love about each other. I love that he is respectable, takes care of himself, and doesn't do drugs or alcohol. Plus he is so clear in his communication style. And those deep blue eyes. . . .

He goes on about my appearance and how much he admires my passion about pursuing a new career. "And at least you're not depressed," he says.

"Oh yes," I agree, thinking about the ups and downs I've faced with my own husband. Mr. Married tells me his wife needs some serious help. Then there's a brief pause, and he says in a calm, steady voice, "My wife is here. She's been listening on the other line. I need to go. I'll talk to you later."

What just happened?! My mind starts spinning. *Have we been found out?* But what did I have to worry about? Of course he'll choose me over her.

Mr. Married tells his wife who I am and that he loves me. He leaves home for a few days to sort things out in his head. When he comes back home, his wife pleads for him to stay. "Don't break up our family. I'll do whatever it takes," she begs. So he stays. For now. I get it, but I know he still loves me. Plus, his marriage has been depressing and unfulfilling for too long. It's only a matter of time, I convince myself.

Barb—Mr. Mister

As executives at the same company, Mr. Mister and I work closely together. I am with him all the time and see him at his best. He's intelligent, in charge, creative—I just love that, you know? I've known him forever. We are good friends and good business partners. I love to watch him work. He loves to watch me in action. People tell me that they can tell we have such respect and admiration for each other in the workplace. That's all it had ever been.

Mr. Mister and I travel a lot together for business. We both enjoy planning for the next trip and travel well together. On a trip to Stockholm, our third colleague who doesn't handle international travel well, goes to bed early on our first night in the city. Neither of us is tired yet, so Mr. Mister and I head to the Spitfire, a quintessential Swedish bar with dark wood paneling and red booths next to the hotel. We drink wine and talk about life. We sit there for hours, sharing our love of business, travel, technology, and purpose. We enjoy that first night so much that we wait for our colleague to turn in early the next night, which he does. We go back to the Spitfire and do the same thing. We connect deeply over our shared interests and mutual respect. We have similar family history. We were both the responsible ones in our families. We are financially independent and successful. We are intellectual equals. We both like structure and rules. And we don't allow people to get too close—although we are letting down our guards with each other little by little.

Often, we are the only two on a work trip, like the long plane ride back to Stockholm a few months later. As usual, we are having an in-depth conversation about our lives and careers. I take off my shoe, pull my foot up onto my knee, and start massaging my foot. Then he reaches over and puts his hand on top of my hand and starts rubbing my foot. I don't expect the excitement that zips through my body as I sit there, drinking a glass of wine with him next to me and his hand touching my foot.

After that, I offer to rub his shoulders. We lift the arm of the seat between us and both turn to sit sideways. As I am rubbing his shoulders, he takes a big deep breath, the kind that you take when you release a bunch of stress—and then I lay my forehead on his back. That was it, that one small gesture. I let down my guard and lean into him, just for a second. We don't say anything about our feelings, but we have just opened Pandora's box.

On our way to our hotel rooms, which are on the same floor, he stops and says, "I want to kiss you so much."

"I want to kiss you too."

Our lips meet and the pulse of attraction and sexual energy runs up through my body, sending my heart into a flutter.

Wait, what are we doing? He's married. I don't do married men. I don't break the rules.

I pull back. "We can't do anything that we can't take back," I say. But I open the door to my room, and we rush in. Sitting on the edge of the bed, gripping each other's hands, the magnitude of the moment floods over us. I continue to say, "We can't do anything we can't take back." We see the choice we are facing. And thankfully, Mr. Mister gets up and walks out the door. We don't break the rules. We don't cross the line. We don't jeopardize our jobs. Yet it is so hard to sleep that night, knowing that he is just on the other side of the wall.

We maintain our physical boundaries. For a few trips. But the tension, the attraction, the pull! He tells me he's been sleeping above the garage at his house for years. I've been separated from Steve for months and know there is no going back to that relationship. Crossing the line with Mr. Mister is inevitable.

The time we spend not having sex creates a force field that becomes impossible to resist. We find ourselves inside my hotel room one night; he is standing behind me, looking at us in the full-length mirror. His arms hold me tight as he kisses the back of my neck. Soon we do what we cannot take back. It is the first night of many together in hotel rooms in faraway cities, pretending that the rest of the world doesn't exist.

It's magical when we can be together. We call it the bubble. When we're traveling, it's like we're living together inside an intense, fun, exciting, fantasy world. Deeper and deeper we go, and each time has an accompanying radical high followed by a devastatingly crushing low. No one can ever know. We can't risk it.

5

—

The Hike

Barb

The weekend after Halloween, Gayle and I meet on a trail that follows a creek through the woods on the outskirts of town. It is a beautiful sunny day. Just as I am getting ready to share, she begins to ask questions. I'm grateful she opens the door to the conversation, because I really need someone to talk to.

"So, you mentioned at dinner you were a little fixated on someone?"

"Well," I hesitate. No one else knows anything about my secret relationship. I'm not one to talk about my feelings with people I don't know well, especially a secret as private as this one, but with Gayle, it seems easy. Talking about my feelings, however, saying them out loud, makes them feel more real. And that is scary.

"We work together," I start. "I think he's brilliant. He thinks the same of me."

"So, who is it? Who is it?" Gayle probes. Her eager excitement doesn't surprise me. She knows some of the people I work with. But I dodge her question.

"I just want to tell you about him," I say.

"Okay, but do I know him?" she insists.

I laugh. "It doesn't really matter who he is. We've worked together for years, and it was always just that. But somehow our work relationship began to grow into a friendship. Everything just feels so easy with him, and at some point, we started to fantasize about what life might be like if we were actually able to be together. And now, he's all I think about."

"Wait. He's married?" Gayle exclaims. "Who is it? Just tell me."

I dodge again and say, "Let's just call him Mr. Mister. He's really unhappy in his marriage, and he doesn't see a way out. He says that he feels like he's in a dark room with no doors or windows. He told me that he can't even think about feeling happy. All he can hope for is that someday he just won't feel so miserable—that neutral is the best he can hope for."

Gayle stops walking, looks directly at me, and fires a penetrating question straight through me. "But, he *is* going to leave, right?"

Everything I've been pushing down starts to bubble up all at once: all of the confusion, the fear, the conflict, the guilt, and the pain. Before I know it, I am telling Gayle everything.

"Even if he did leave, there is no way we could both stay at the company. Neither one of us is willing to give up our career, and the CEO would never, never, never allow us to stay in our leadership positions while having a romantic relationship. Basically, I'm trapped."

"So . . . it's someone you work with *and* he's married?" Gayle is still focused on figuring out who it is. She continues guessing, and each name becomes more absurd than the one before. "Is it Joe?" Gayle asks.

"No way. Are you kidding? Not Joe. I can't believe you would even say that—we are so different."

"Is it Bill?" she says.

The suggestion of Bill brings an even longer *nooooo*. My relationship with Mr. Mister has lived inside a bubble that only the two of us are in. As soon as I say his name out loud, that bubble will no longer be ours alone. Plus, Gayle knows him, which will increase the risk of my secret getting out.

"Stop," I finally say but wonder if it would feel good to admit it out loud. *Why not?* I figure. I trust her. She won't tell anyone; I know that.

I tell her who it is and immediately feel the tension leave my body.

"Ohhh, that makes sense. I can see how the two of you would be so good together. But how can you be with him if he's not leaving?" Gayle adds. "He really does seem unhappy. But why isn't he going to leave? I can't believe he would stay with her when he can have you." Gayle is stunned. "How could you be with someone who's not going to leave? I can't imagine that."

"Yeah, exactly," I tell her. "I've never been attracted to a married man—I don't like to share. But this situation feels so different. The intensity when I am with him is like the best drug ever. I feel so alive. I get caught in the cycle of being with him, wanting a life with him, realizing that he'll never change his circumstances, and then diving into the depths of despair. It's like being on the most nauseating, exhausting treadmill with no way off.

"The first thing I do when I get home from work is open up my laptop and wait for the 'ding' of his text messages and his nightly phone calls when he's retired to the room above the garage. That is our way of being alone together, of feeling like the reality of our situation doesn't exist. We take tons of precautions, of course; like, no saved messages, ever. . . . Ugh, I don't know. It's so fucked up. It's literally the *most* fucked up situation I can imagine. And yet, I stick around. What the fuck is wrong with me?"

"What do you mean what's wrong with you? He's the one who's not leaving. That's crazy. So, start from the beginning. How did all this happen?" Gayle asks.

As I tell Gayle my story, I notice that telling her the truth is opening my awareness. The whole relationship with Mr. Mister starts to feel incredibly fucked up. *Why am I so focused on a future with him when he isn't focused on a future with me?* I find myself wondering. *And, wait a minute—I don't do married men. So why am I obsessing over this one?* Then I recall the saying that an affair is a ladder out of a marriage. "Have you ever heard of that saying?" I ask Gayle. She responds with a quick, "No but it makes sense, especially if you feel stuck and can't see a way out."

After that hike, Gayle and I hang out regularly and share the "fucked-upness" of our respective situations. Our dinners at Lefty's become weekly events that are interspersed with walks along the creek and long, long talks. We talk about everything—our inner worlds and our secrets. Our conversations are surprisingly effortless given how new our friendship at this level really is. I feel so comfortable sharing my fears and secrets openly with Gayle. I am amazed by how nice it is to not feel alone—and a man has nothing to do with it.

Pretty quickly, Gayle and I become one another's safe space. We share a long history of self-help, spiritual seeking, therapy, and a strong desire to evolve into more whole people—although our blind spots are our relationships with men. My back deck becomes our haven to work out our shit. Little do we know that our blind spots are about to see the light of day.

"I've never had a friendship like this," I tell her. "I've spent my life being independent and self-sufficient. It's nice to have someone to really talk to." I've always been guarded, but in Gayle, I have found a new kind of connection and it's not scaring me away.

Gayle smiles back. "It's nice for me too."

6

How Did We Get Here?

Barb

I have always been independent. I began my first job as a waitress the very day I was eligible for a work permit at fifteen-and-a-half years old. Before we opened for breakfast, I'd gather the other servers and say, "Let's see who can make the most money today," because the only way you make money as a waitress is if you're really good at what you do. The need for financial independence was deeply engrained in me. I witnessed my mother's struggle to make ends meet as a single mother of three small children. She held two jobs and managed the apartment building that we lived in. Her parents, who lived nearby, served as our primary caregivers. She modeled that when shit hit the fan, everything else was put on hold and you went to work.

When my father abandoned the family, I remember my mother and me standing at the bedroom window as his car backed down the driveway. In a matter-of-fact tone she said, "He will never be back." At just two years old, I had no reaction; I simply continued to stare out the window, unable to comprehend what she had just said. Therapy helped me understand how that early lesson created a silent but deeply held belief that I was not worthy of a man's love.

By the time I was twenty-seven, I was married to my high

school sweetheart and was the mother of a toddler. I blamed my husband for not being enough—not deep enough or spiritual enough. One day, I remember sitting on the floor next to a pile of laundry with my legs folded underneath me. As I folded each piece of clothing, I began to realize the depth of my sadness and just how long I had been feeling it. Suddenly, I thought, *This is what it's like to lose your mind. I wonder if I'm on the edge of a mental breakdown.* I felt like I needed to escape my marriage but didn't know why. We were young, and after twelve years together, it felt too hard to keep it going. The story I made up was that my husband was incapable of meeting my needs, so I convinced myself that I had to leave in order to save my own life. Strike one for finding a man to fix and fulfill me.

In truth, I wanted to find a different man. I knew a wounded part of me needed to be healed, and I subconsciously thought the right man would fix me.

Around the same time, a friend told me she had learned about the twelve-step program Adult Children of Alcoholics (alcoholism runs in my family). I decided to go with her. In that meeting, I felt found for the first time. I felt hope for a way out of my suffering. Then, through the pain of the divorce, I began to go to therapy. Those two avenues started me toward self-awareness, put me on my spiritual path, and helped me to see how fucked up my relationships with men were.

After our separation, I got involved in a string of meaningless relationships, one incompatible pairing after another. Each of these would last about six months. As soon as I felt the guy pulling away, I would run. At the time, my strategy felt perfect. Even though I could take care of my son, Brent, and myself,

I knew I wasn't good at being alone. Always having a man to hold on to prevented that. At one point, I had a man I traveled with on weekend road trips and to Mexico, a man I could have deep meaningful conversations with about my workday and my kid, and a man I had great sex with. I was obsessed with each one of these men while we were together. When something uncomfortable would happen, I would end it. I did this over and over until I met my second husband, Steve.

Steve was six-foot-five with dark hair and blue eyes. He was kind, warm-hearted, easygoing, and super athletic. He didn't have a drive like I did for financial independence and a career; he was content to live simply. Although he was really good at what he did (physical training, bodywork, etc.), he wasn't committed to a career like I was. I was in my thirties when we met. We spent a lot of time together and, eventually, he moved into the house I'd bought after my divorce. It was the first time I thought I had found a relationship that would last forever. I became committed to the idea that, no matter what, we would work out our differences, whatever they might be. A year later, we were married at my family's lake house in the Sierra Nevada Mountains, and our daughter, Sammy, was born shortly thereafter.

Over the years, as our marriage hit its inevitable rough spots, I eventually found my new focus, working to make him happy. I would probe like the best therapist until I discovered what was in the way of him feeling self-expressed and happy, and I would support his movement toward it. I don't recall if he ever really asked for my help, but I was on the job! He'd start to feel dissatisfied, I'd go to work to fix it, he'd start to make some changes, and things would improve a bit.

But eventually, his unhappiness would resurface, and the cycle would once again begin. I wanted him to be successful, independent, and motivated . . . like me.

One of the ways I tried to make him happy was to buy a sixteen-acre ranch outside of town for us to renovate and develop. That ranch became a painful part of our history—I bit off more than *he* could chew, as it was overwhelming and far away from everything. Eventually, I realized that he needed to find happiness in himself—this was his challenge, not mine. I shut down emotionally and just powered through each day, focusing on my own career and desires. I convinced myself that I needed more space, so I moved to the downstairs bedroom. After several months of this, I decided it was time to move out. Strike two. Today, I realize that my need to fix the men in my life was born out of my need to have a man who could give me what I needed to feel seen, safe, and secure.

I started to look for houses that were closer to town, my job, and my daughter's school. By this point, my son, Brent, was a young adult and already out of the house. One night at dinner, a girlfriend told me about a cute little artist's bungalow that was coming on the market. Within two days, I'd seen it and made an offer. Soon my daughter and I were all settled in our new little sanctuary while Steve stayed behind at the ranch.

The house was exactly what I needed to heal my confused and sad heart. In front, there was a fence covered in jasmine and lined with Japanese maple trees. I always felt like I was walking down a winding path into a secret garden. The charm of this 1,000-square-foot, two-bedroom house welcomed me as soon as I came through the door. Cozy and warm, the original wood floors and double-hung windows reflected a time gone by. The back deck was made of ironwood with hand-made iron spindles that looked like grape vines and ran the length of the house. The deck sat beneath a wisteria-framed pergola set perfectly against a forest that served as the back-yard. It was a beautiful and calming home to ground me as I moved through the ending of marriage number two.

The move to my little sanctuary was a first step away from Steve, but for the most part, we continued to operate as a family. We didn't even talk about divorce for a few years; there was no driving force for either one of us to officially end it. When Steve finally suggested it, it simply seemed like the practical choice. Our daughter was the common thread that tied us together. We still co-parented, traveled to her basketball games together, and shared our golden retriever, Zoey. He was the second husband whom I blamed for not meeting my needs. Neither husband had matched my ambition or my drive for financial security and, most important, my spiritual quest for a deep connection. No matter how much I blamed them for the problems in our marriages, I was starting to see that the common denominator wasn't them; it was me.

What seemed so hard to see before I moved out was now becoming clear. It was always me. My emotional needs were never going to be met by a man until I was really okay with me . . . being me. But my obsession with Mr. Mister kept me from coming face to face with that truth.

Every other week, when Sammy was with her dad, I was free. With that freedom came more entanglement with Mr. Mister. Soon he absorbed my life. We were in constant communication. He would come over after work for a glass of wine. The energy between us was so electric. We would work together during the day, and then I would crave seeing him or talking with him each night. We knew the potential consequences of being found out, but that made it even more exciting.

At times, I would try to come to my senses, remind myself that "I don't do married men," and distract myself with someone else. Soon there were several: Steve who I didn't feel connected with, but with whom my life was still entangled; a former lover, John, who had relocated to our little town; as well as a delicious artist who was curious and unlike anyone I'd experienced. My plate was full, but was I happy? I was not. I was weary. Weary of the on-again, off-again nature of my relationships and the secrecy with Mr. Mister. Weary of hoping one man would fix me only to find out he could not.

I met the artist while out with my girlfriends at a local restaurant. He walked up and stood next to me as I was ordering a cocktail at the bar. "What's your name?" he asked.

"Barb," I told him. "And you are?"

"I'm Jackson."

He was gorgeous with his brown wavy hair and blue eyes, and he exuded confidence and calmness.

"What do you do?" my overdeveloped-professional-woman self asked.

"I'm a painter," he responded.

"A painter?" I asked as I motioned my hand up and down as if painting a house. "Or a fine art painter?"

"The latter." We flirted throughout the evening, and as we were leaving the restaurant, he stopped, embraced me, and slowly moved me backward until I was up against the brick building. We made out like teenagers. Feeling the desire of someone else felt good, and he was charming and mysterious. He piqued my interest. A brief but intense fling followed that evening. I attached more meaning to it than was appropriate. That became apparent when, out with friends Hollie and Gayle for dinner, I saw him walk into the restaurant hand in hand with another woman. This, after he had made an excuse as to why we weren't going to get together that night. I felt a sense of panic, like I was going to burst into tears.

"We're leaving right now," I barked to the girls. "Right now!" And we did. Back at home with Gayle, I immediately took off my clothes, put on my red robe, and proceeded to throw myself down on the couch, sobbing uncontrollably into the couch pillows.

You might think this disappointment would have slowed me down, but shortly after that, I was back in the saddle. After a friendly dinner with my former lover John, we went back to his place for a glass of wine. We'd dated after my first divorce. He was fifteen years my senior and someone who cared deeply about me. He was the first person who really showed me what caring looked like. He would drop by with groceries or offer to help with my then-young son, anything to help ease my burden. After moving to another state for nearly twenty years, he'd returned to retire nearby. We reconnected and enjoyed a friendship. That evening at his house, he told me that he wanted more from me. I told him that I wasn't available for a romantic relationship with him because there was someone else in my life and that relationship was a secret. I told him all about Mr. Mister.

John then asked me a question that still makes my heart

stop: "What would you do if Mr. Mister called you right now and told you he was in London and asked you to come meet him there?"

I looked right at him and without even thinking and with absolute clarity said, "If that happened, I would get on the next plane and meet him wherever he was." In that moment, I knew the truth. Mr. Mister was the only man I wanted, and he was the only one I could not have.

I had created the space to be fully free. I had a career that provided financial independence, I had time to travel how and when I wanted, and I could date whomever I chose. Sammy and I were living in our lovely little sanctuary. My inner connection to spirit, which had begun with years of twelve-step programs followed by work with a few great therapists and many spiritual teachers, was strong. My spiritual seeking even opened me to a new awareness that brought me a few moments of feeling enlightened.

I had a preoccupation with anything and everything "self-help." I had a practice of reading books, journaling questions to myself, and waiting for answers. Even I realized the extent of my compulsion when one day, as I was standing in front of the Self-Help section in my local bookstore, I thought, *If I could only read every single one of these books on these shelves, then I would be healed.* That search took many forms. Counseling, spiritual teaching, and self-help books helped me to identify my "original wound" of being abandoned by my father.

So much of my life was working because these spiritual resources were helping me make sense of the confusion and weariness, but I still had this profound, underlying anxiety about not having the "right" man in my life. The more awareness I gained, the more I suffered. The truth is that awareness is only one step. Awareness can come through reading and listening, but change only comes through action. As I began to see the dependency I was living with, I felt more and more pain. Why was I so psychologically and chemically addicted to these toxic man cycles? I knew I needed to make a radical change to break free.

When I felt the anxiety rise, I would think, *Who am I to complain? Who am I to feel down about my life? I have it pretty good.* And I did. From the outside, my life looked like it was under control, but my inner life was a wild mess. The energy I was spending, the anxiety I felt, and the obsession I lived with were all, quite literally, driving me crazy. The only thing I believed would bring the peace I sought would be to find that one, right man. Someone to dream about a future with. Someone to get excited about. Someone to spend time with. Someone to work on a relationship with. Someone to distract me from my deep aloneness and the depth of my sadness.

In those moments, I so desperately wanted that to be Mr. Mister. He was the first man I truly felt connected to. We shared so many of the same loves: business, travel, leadership, accomplishment. I was open with him, and he saw who I really was. Our personal interactions touched that place in my heart that needed to be healed. Of course, he must be the one to fill that aching hole.

As Gayle and I deepened our renewed friendship, we often sat together on my secluded back deck, curled up on the outdoor sectional, talking for hours about where our lives were, how to heal them, and where we wanted to go. We could see we were stuck. We knew where we wanted to go, but we didn't know how to get there. Eventually, our hunger for spiritual direction would lead us to the answer we both needed—although it wouldn't be the one we expected.

Gayle

For me, like with Barb, my pattern with men also started with my dad. He taught me that it was important to be the perfect wife and mother and what to look for in a man, one that was a good provider. I grew up in the 1970s in a traditional household in idyllic Marin County, California. My dad drove across the Golden Gate Bridge each morning to work as the senior vice president of Wells Fargo. We were always financially secure; I knew my dad would provide for us. Our life was very stable. My model for family and love was that the man left for work each day and returned home at exactly the same time each evening to the dinner my stay-at-home mom had prepared for him. Though my dad never showed physical affection, he gave his attention and approval when I did well in school, excelled at sports, and kept up my physical appearance. My parents valued the external much more than the internal; looks and social status took precedence over personal feelings and needs, which we never even discussed.

When I was fifteen, I read a book that deeply influenced the way I saw love. Judy Blume's *Forever . . .* is a 1975 novel that tells the story of first love and teenage sexuality. I so identified with Katherine, the protagonist who believed that when she had sex with Michael, it would seal their love "forever." But their relationship ends when Katherine goes to work at an out-of-state summer camp. I remember being shocked that the book ended that way because the title was literally

Forever . . . , and I naively thought that when you met someone, fell in love, and had sex with them, you would be together forever. I recall making the conscious decision then and there that when I fell in love, it would be forever. Nothing would tear us apart.

Not long after reading that book, I got my first serious boyfriend, Chris. He gave me an engagement ring when I was sixteen, much to my parents' dismay. Even though we weren't planning a wedding any time soon, just the fact that I wore an engagement ring was upsetting enough for my parents to seek family therapy.

When my parents announced that we would be moving to Florida when I was seventeen and a junior in high school, I refused to go with them. By then I was opinionated and strong-willed. Plus, I wasn't about to leave my boyfriend-fiancé. I knew what I wanted, and I was going to figure out how to get it (what my friends and family call Gayle-force). Determined to get my way, I came up with a plan to move in with a family who lived down the street and become their live-in housekeeper/babysitter. I convinced the family whom I wanted to live with that this would be good for them, and I made it clear to my parents that I was not going to leave.

Finally, the therapist told my parents that forcing me to leave would cause irreparable damage to our relationship. They eventually agreed and moved to Florida without me. Even though I was the one who refused to move with my family, I still felt abandoned when they relocated to the other side of the country. This caused me to become even more dependent on my boyfriend-fiancé, whom I was determined to be with forever.

By this time, I was pretty much over high school. My good grades and summer school credits meant that I was able to graduate a semester early. After a semester at the College of Marin, I went off to Chico State University where I moved in and played house with Chris. My parents, especially my dad, were very much against me living with Chris, but they valued education so much that they still paid the costs of my books and tuition. Chris and my student loan basically provided for everything else.

The thought that my parents disapproved of me living with Chris weighed heavily on my desire to please them. And I was getting bored with Chris. On a summer trip to Florida to visit them, I met someone else, and my teenage mind decided that what I really needed was freedom to be with whomever I wanted. My parents were thrilled when I ended up transferring to Florida State University. When my relationship with Chris ended, they began to fully support me financially all the way through grad school, where I studied psychology.

I have always been fascinated by the dynamics of relationships. My master's thesis, "Long Term Soap Opera Viewers' Perceptions of Reality," statistically showed that people like me, who were addicted to watching soap operas, had distorted perceptions of romantic relationships. I am a prime example of this phenomenon.

During my last year of grad school, in order to gain more experience, and for a little extra spending money, I took a job as a psychiatrist's assistant in a teaching hospital. It was there that I met my dream husband. Greg was a tall, blond-haired, blue-eyed, fourth-year med student who was there to do a monthlong psych rotation as part of his medical school program. I could tell by the way he interacted with the child patients in the hospital that he would make a wonderful father.

We fell madly in love, were engaged within six months, and married six months later. When my dad walked me down the aisle on that warm June day and "gave me away" to my husband, my soulmate, I felt like we were one and would stay that way for all eternity. I was living my own Disney princess, soap opera–fueled fantasy. My wedding day was the first time my dad told me that he loved me, so you can imagine the hole I had felt inside me.

We moved to Grand Rapids, Michigan, and then to Columbus, Ohio, where Greg finished his first residency, and we had our first child within two years. I became a stay-at-home mom, while Greg stepped right into the role of provider, and two more children quickly followed, echoing the tradition of my own childhood. Early in our marriage, though, Greg's love of partying became apparent and created tension throughout our years together. Yet I had these ideal visions of our life where I never had to work and we would go to formal events where I looked my best with Greg beside me in his suit. When our youngest was nine, we built our forever home: 3,800 square feet of custom woodwork, marble fireplaces, floor-to-ceiling windows, and landscaped gardens. From the outside life looked idyllic, until it wasn't.

On January 10, 2001, a friend called to tell me that there was an active shooter at the mental health clinic where Greg worked. My heart was beating out of my chest, and the room was spinning. Searching for details, I turned on the local radio station and learned that the gunman was a patient at the clinic and was still on the loose. We lived within walking distance of the clinic, and I could hear the helicopters overhead searching for the gunman. I immediately tried to call Greg, but he didn't answer.

He wasn't at the clinic that day; he was at his private practice office close by. I kept trying to reach him, thinking the gunman was a patient of his and could be heading to his private office to kill him. Realizing that Greg was likely with a patient, I jumped in the car and drove to his office, burst into his session, and screamed that he needed to get out of the office right now. When he saw my panic, he understood how bad the situation was, grabbed his briefcase, and went home with me.

Later we would learn that the gunman killed two people at the clinic and several more were injured when they jumped from a second-story window trying to escape. He then went to a local restaurant, killed another man, and wounded others before the police apprehended him the following day. Greg seemed to be detached from the trauma. We went to the memorial service for the young intern who was killed in his clinic, and it struck me that Greg didn't cry. In contrast, I sobbed uncontrollably.

Three months later, a group of women from his office rented a limo for Greg's birthday and took him out drinking. I had no knowledge of the party, nor was I invited. Greg came home four hours later than anticipated, and he was very, very drunk. Bouncing off the hallway walls on his way to our bedroom, he fell on top of the bed and passed out. It wasn't the first time I'd seen him this way, but it became more frequent.

Soon, Greg would wake up every morning and vomit in the shower like I'd done through each of my pregnancies.

He became ghostly and clammy. He would wake up in a panic from nightmares. However, there were moments of hope over the next few years when he would quit drinking. His eyes weren't bloodshot anymore, and he was present with me again. His kind-hearted, generous, and funny nature would resurface; we'd have guests over, and he'd make his famous barbecue. That was the man I fell in love with.

Then the relapses would come. One morning, Greg vomited and came back to bed, too sick to work. It was then that he admitted that he might have a problem and called a close friend who was in recovery. I also made the decision not to drink for a while. I realized that I had developed my own coping mechanism, wine, something I would reach for to ease my own suffering. I joined Al-Anon, stopped drinking half bottles of Chardonnay in front of the TV every night, and patiently supported my husband. The racks that filled our new wine cellar and the wine fridge I'd just purchased to keep our collection of whites at the perfect temperature sat empty.

When I stopped drinking, I began to see myself more clearly—where my life was out of alignment with reality. What I started doing out of respect for Greg turned into doing something out of respect for myself. I could see how in our relationship, I had always wanted to be a priority, but never was. I was always in the background. There had been no sense of a "we" for years, so I began to work on myself. Al-Anon, therapy, and even a women's Bible study group helped me begin to see my part in all of it and how controlling I was. The more I became self-aware, the more I wanted to feel connected, have freedom, and become authentically me.

The night I discovered Greg had a girlfriend, I sat in my

big, beautiful bed all alone in shock. I heard a buzzing in my head; I was still shaking and couldn't tell if I was hot or cold. Greg and I had an intense day where he gaslit me—turning everything back toward me. He was angry with me for reading the text messages; he was angry because I had told other people and even that I had called a friend to come pick up the kids.

Through all of that, I began to hear a voice in my head: *I am worthy of a healthy marriage. I deserve a man who will love me. I deserve exclusivity in my marriage. I deserve a husband who makes his relationship with me a top priority. I deserve a husband who really wants me and wants to be with me forever. I deserve a husband who does not abuse alcohol, so when he's with me, he's actually present.*

No doubt those affirmations came from all the self-help reading I'd been doing. But that voice was quickly followed by, *I don't want to lose him. I don't want him to leave me, but I feel like he is already gone.* The second voice inside me told me I'd be alone, which scared me more than the voice that was trying to fight for my worth. I would rather work it out with Greg than start all over with someone new. I knew this much about myself: I was not meant to be alone.

A week later, because neither of us wanted to go through a divorce, we came to an emotionless agreement to stay married under the conditions that he would no longer see the girlfriend or drink and party to excess.

But Greg never lived up to the agreement we made.

Four years later I said the D-word out loud. Greg and I had been living separate lives in the same house, rarely connecting for four years. He had been sleeping downstairs in the guest quarters for almost a year, and I had been convincing myself things would be fine. Until I went skydiving.

In October just before I reconnected with Barb, Greg confronted me during an argument. "Just say it! Just say it, Gayle!" he yelled at me. It was one of those moments that is still frozen in my mind. "Just say what you want!"

We were standing face to face, about four feet apart in our massive travertine marble bathroom. I looked into his vacant, bloodshot, blue eyes, and somehow found the strength to say the inevitable words out loud— the truth—the words that I vowed to myself, to God, and to my husband I would never utter: "I want a divorce."

Like toothpaste that's left the tube, those words could not be put back. Some say that what stands between you and freedom is a five-minute, sweaty-palmed conversation. For me, that felt true. The shocked look on Greg's face reflected the shock I felt inside. I had put up with so much toxic behavior during the last few years, that I think he truly believed I would never leave him. Those four words, "I want a divorce," were ones I never fathomed would come out of my mouth. I did not "believe" in divorce. Divorce wasn't something that people in my family did. I believed in commitment and never considered divorce an option.

"But I was really looking forward to the day the kids were all out of the house, and I could have you all to myself," he lied.

"That's bullshit," I said. "I've heard from more than one person that your plan was to leave as soon as the kids were gone." Even though I was the one to first speak the D-word out loud, I knew he had been planning to leave me all along as soon as our last child graduated high school.

The heaviness and dread that had been growing in and between us for nearly a decade was finally released. We agreed to keep the news to ourselves for the time being; it felt overwhelming. I had just started grad school for a second master's degree so that I could become a licensed family therapist in California. We would have to sell the house. We would have to tell the kids. Our girls, Sierra and Carley, were away at college, and our son, Cody, was busy being the captain of his high school football team and spent most of his time either at school or at friends' homes. We waited several months before we shared our plan with them and others. Slowly, Greg began to move things out of our house into a small place less than fifteen minutes away. I was so used to his unpredictable coming and going that not much seemed to change.

Finally, we did the preliminary work to put our house on the market, and I began looking for a rental of my own. The timing wasn't great as far as the housing market was concerned, but now that we had called it, there was no going back.

I wasn't sure how I was going to do this on my own, though I still hoped Mr. Married would be there waiting for me. In reality, he wasn't moving any closer to leaving his wife. I thought maybe I had made a terrible mistake. But, at my core, I knew two things with great clarity: no matter what happened with Mr. Married, my marriage to Greg was over, and I believed deep down that life was too short to stay so unhappy. I was no longer afraid of a different life.

$$7$$

Lights Out

Barb

One Sunday morning at 7:30, Gayle sends me a text: "Hi, I want to come over and drink coffee with you on your back deck." I'm surprised she is awake so early. She's not known for being a morning person, but I don't hesitate. "Come on over."

Gayle is at my place in minutes.

"I don't think I have ever seen you up this early!" I say with a smile as she comes inside.

"I know, but I woke up and felt this calling, like a pull, to get out of bed and come straight here. It almost felt like a message from above to have my morning coffee with you on this magical wisteria-covered deck." She laughs as she sits down.

Gayle

I can't really explain why I woke up so early and felt compelled to come to Barb's this morning, but I follow the impulse anyway. Her deck has a sacred, comfortable, home-base vibe that is heightened whenever we are there together. All I can say is I'm trying to pay more attention to my inner guidance.

We lounge in Barb's new, comfy, sectional wicker sofa and sip our morning coffee. It's a beautiful sunny spring morning, and the periwinkle wisteria is in bloom above us. Barb is in her red velour robe, and I am in the yoga pants and hooded sweatshirt I'd thrown on before jetting out of my place.

Barb and I are incredibly close at this point, six months after our reconnection on Halloween night. We've discovered a truly authentic and intimate relationship with one another despite our outward differences. Inwardly, we share so much in common: love for good food and wine, desire for personal growth, interest in spiritual exploration. Over the last six months, Barb and I have talked for hours about the habits we gained from our respective family systems. We both had fathers who were unavailable. So it was only natural that we would eventually find ourselves attracted to men who were not only emotionally unavailable but *who were also married*. The only future we had with these men existed in our imaginations, fueled with hope but without evidence of any clear action.

This morning, we bond over the fact that we both feel lost. We both feel depleted by our respective men. We both want authentic lives. And we both feel powerless to change.

I begin to share the dream I had the night before. "I was floating in the sparkling, sun-soaked, Mexican ocean with my longtime friend, Asha." I add some context for Barb's understanding. "In real life, Asha left her life in Portland to begin an entirely new life as a facilitator of Ibogaine at her ex-husband's clinic, The Dream House in San Pancho, Mexico."

"What's Ibogaine?" Barb asks.

"From what I understand, it's a strong hallucinogenic medicine from an African root plant that's used to treat serious addictions. It's illegal in the States. Asha's clinic is the same one Greg checked himself into six months ago, right when you and I first reconnected," I say.

"Wow," Barb says. "That's crazy!"

"I know, right?!" I exclaim. "Now, when Greg went down there, his hope was to work through his deep-rooted physical and psychological issues. While there, he took off his wedding ring and left it behind on his nightstand at the clinic. He told me later, in his post-Ibogaine 'guru state,' 'It means nothing to me. I am not attached to it.' He had been attached to alcohol and other women for decades, but his wedding ring was apparently far too burdensome. The truth was that it broke my heart. Even though we had already decided to get divorced, seeing his naked finger without that gold band on it after twenty-two years hurt like hell."

As I tell her about my personally significant Asha dream, my phone rings. It's Asha! I haven't heard from her in nine months, but now, the moment I mention her, here she is. "Asha, hi. I was just telling my girlfriend about a dream I had about you last night!"

Asha replies with her own shock: "No way, I was calling to tell you about a dream I had about you last night!"

"We must really be connected on a spiritual level. Really incredible synchronicity-type shit happening," I say.

"Totally!"

Suddenly, I hear a terrifying series of sounds: three distinct thuds, followed immediately by a frightening scream from Barb's daughter: "GAYLE!!!"

I drop my phone and run inside. What I see next is horrifying. Barb, in her red velour robe, is face down on her hallway floor. She is so stiff, still, and awkwardly positioned that I am sure she is dead.

Sammy is frozen in shock, staring down at her mom's body.

I go straight into emergency mode. "Everything is going to be all right, but I need you to call 9-1-1."

Sam doesn't move. "Sammy, call 9-1-1," I bark.

She seems to hear me this time and begins to travel at what feels like a sloth's pace toward the phone.

Shit! I berate myself internally. *I should have taken that CPR class all those years ago! I have no idea what to do.* I kneel down to check for a pulse and see if Barb is still breathing. *That's what people do in these situations, right?* I am very much grasping at straws. 9-1-1 isn't answering. *Why aren't they answering?*

My mind is racing.

"Come on, Barb, wake up," I plead. You are not supposed to move a person after an accident because you could re-injure their broken neck or back or something, right?

I lean in to touch Barb's still, motionless face when she suddenly jolts awake! She gasps for air, and her eyes fly open, wild, terrified, and confused.

"Holy shit, that was scary. Are you all right?" I ask.

Barb

I get off the couch and walk inside while Gayle takes her phone call. I pass Sammy, who is watching Sunday morning TV in the living room. As I turn the corner into the bathroom, I begin to feel a strange sensation. I have a quick passing thought. *Hmm, what is that?* I wonder—and everything stops.

The next thing I remember is hearing Gayle's voice. Sammy tells me that I grabbed on to the sides of the bathroom doorjamb, attempting to steady myself, but that I fell backward, hitting the wall on the other side of the hallway and then collapsing into a heap on the floor.

Gayle's voice is calm and clear. She is speaking slowly and clearly so Sammy can understand and stay calm.

When I come to a bit more, we move back out to the deck. Checking in with my body, I realize I am beginning to feel better.

"Wow, that was weird, huh?" I say to Gayle. Then, suddenly, I feel it coming on again. The strange sensation in my belly, followed by an odd feeling in my head that makes it impossible to communicate, and then I am out. Again.

A few minutes later, after a third incident, we decide we need help, so we call my husband. Steve is the one who always handles medical issues in our family, and soon he is sitting next to me on the couch, taking stock of the situation. Then it happens again—darkness, out. Gayle stays with my daughter, Steve scoops me up, and away we go to the local emergency room.

I feel relieved when I see my boss's best friend, Brad, who is an ER doc, smiling at me from the foot of my bed. He is the head of the emergency department, so I know I am in good hands. The medical staff hooks me up to what feels like dozens of machines and starts an IV. The ER team stands and watches as I report the funny feeling in my gut, which is followed by another spell. Soon I am awake again, and we carry on, them interviewing me, me trying to stay conscious long enough to answer their questions.

"Barb," Dr. Brad begins, "can you tell me what you have eaten recently? Are you taking any medications? Anything abnormal about your urine or bowel movements?"

Dammit! I think. *Why did he have to ask me about that?* Dr. Brad is one of those handsome doctors who always has a ready smile and warm hello. I don't want him knowing about my bowel movements!

"Well, hmm, umm, yes, I noticed a little something red this morning," I cringe. *Ugh! What I would give for a doctor I don't know in this moment!* I think the redness is probably just remnants of the beets I'd eaten a night or two before, but I know I have to tell him. Gratefully, my brain fog allows me to be totally honest, but my ego quickly kicks back into gear after the words leave my mouth. *Why did you tell him that?*

As these words are dashing around my foggy brain, Dr. Brad leans over, looks right at me with his kind, warm eyes, and says, "You know, I'm going to have to check that out."

"Of course you are," I groan in embarrassment.

The good news about being in such a fog is that the humiliation I would normally feel over Dr. Brad checking out my nether regions is significantly lower than it would be had I been totally lucid. Dr. Brad discovers, gratefully, that the problem down south is merely a bulging hemorrhoid, and we are able to put that part of my testing to rest, though it doesn't explain why I'm passing out.

With no ready answers, he admits me to the hospital. My team of doctors grows to include a neurologist, a cardiologist, and an internist. I have test after test after test after test (EEG, EKG, urinalysis). Steve stays by my side; but no Mr. Mister. No visit, no text, no phone call. The next day, when the CEO of the company comes to visit me, I know that Mr. Mister knows I'm in the hospital; but still nothing. His absence makes me feel so sad, so lost on top of the fear about the medical mystery I am in the throes of. Even with the fogginess and the commotion around me, I can't get Mr. Mister out of my mind. I lay in that hospital bed and think, *I could be dying, and you don't even care enough to come see me. What must I mean to you? Do I not even matter?* Those questions receive the same answer as all the others. He doesn't visit me, even in the hospital, because he is married—fucker!

After a few days in the hospital, the doctor sends me home with a change to my migraine medications, but no smoking guns are found. It feels good to be able to take a few days off and rest. I hadn't realized it, but I am exhausted. My life has become stressful and, although I have no answers as to the cause of these mysterious fainting spells, I am glad to be able to take a break. With rest, my strength increases, and I begin to feel more like myself again.

One afternoon a few days later, my friend Hollie comes over to check on me. As I see her come down the walkway toward my door with her familiar welcoming smile, I definitely recognize her, but I cannot, for the life of me, remember her name. Immediately my whole body is filled with panic.

I know her. I know her, I repeat to myself.

My mind is racing. I know her name as well as I know my own, but I can't find it in my memory. I look at her and say, "Hi," but there is a pregnant pause as I try to find her name. Hollie sees me struggling and helps me out.

"Hollie," she says with more than a little concern in her voice. Hollie calls Gayle, who appears at my door in minutes. Hollie, Gayle, and I huddle up together in the kitchen, thinking the same thought simultaneously: *What the hell is going on?*

We decide the best thing to do is to call Gayle's psychiatrist, soon-to-be ex-husband. Reluctantly, Gayle dials, and we follow his advice. Greg, in his assuring West Virginia accent, says, "The rule in medicine is you need to get to a baseline." He suggests I stop taking all the medications for migraines I have been prescribed, so they can get a baseline read on my brain function. I make a subsequent appointment with my neurologist; he agrees and schedules a head and neck MRI.

A few days later, I am getting my MRI. My technician, who seems nice enough, looks directly at me and with a very firm voice says, "Here's what's going to happen. When I tell you to, you're going to lay down and close your eyes, and you're not going to open them until I tell you to. It'll be about seventeen minutes. But you have to promise me that once you close your eyes, you won't open them again until I say. Got it?"

I reply with a compliant, "Yes ma'am." I lay on the table, close my eyes, and hear a click, click, click sound as she places a cage over my head so I cannot move. She rolls me into the MRI tube that is barely larger than my body, and all I can think about is the fact that my head is pinned to a table and my entire body is inside this really fucking small tube. I know I can't freak out because that will make the whole experience even scarier, so I go to my happy place and pretend that none of this is actually happening. As I feel the machine pull me in, I focus on the music in the background and proceed to disassociate from my body. I imagine myself floating freely in space. The air is cool, and the sun is bright. There is no Earth, no buildings, and no sky. There is just infinite space, no boundaries.

A couple of days later, I am feeling well enough to return to work. It is a relief to have my days scheduled. I run a business unit, so there is always a lot to do. That day, I am meeting with our CEO and Mr. Mister himself. Although he had eventually texted to check on me, I am still pissed. However, like usual, I set aside those feelings and focus on working as a team. I am sitting in the conference room with the two of them across the conference table from me, and a blackout starts to happen again. I look up at them as they begin to zoom backward away from me. It is as if I am sitting in a chair that is quickly being pulled away from the table. I stop talking, hoping it will pass, but eventually realize I have to ask them to get me help.

Back at my doctor's office, she asks me the common first questions: What am I eating? Am I drinking enough fluids? On and on. The MRI had shown nothing. My responses must have a casual tone because she looks hard at me with her hand on her hip, and in her most stern voice says, "This issue, whatever is going on, is important. It is the most important thing in your life in this moment. It is more important than work and more important than what's going on in your family. This is your health we're talking about. You can't work right now, you can't drive right now, and you have to pay attention!"

With the words "you can't work," she crushes me. I am devastated, shocked. *Not work? What? This can't be!* In this brief moment, I go from being someone who is capable, in charge, and empowered to someone who is completely broken, vulnerable, and frightened beyond words. I sob as I think that without work, I'm nothing, and work, of course, is where Mr. Mister is.

I am officially on a leave of absence. Zero work is the order. None, zip, zilch. While the reality leaves me feeling socially and psychologically untethered, the truth is, physically and emotionally, I don't feel much like working anyway.

8

Dr. J

Barb

At home, a couple of days later, I try to relax. Being disconnected from the world is refreshing. Then my phone dings. Lost in a spacious life free of back-to-back meetings, I have forgotten what it's like to be ruled by my calendar. I had forgotten about the appointment with Dr. J, an Ayurvedic practitioner from Sri Lanka, whom I'd met at a dinner a month before at my friend Teri's house. Ayurveda is a traditional Indian and homeopathic approach to living, and Dr. J was as mysterious as he was charming. Before I left dinner that evening, I found him so spiritually inspiring that I'd scheduled a session with him.

My initial reaction now is to cancel. After all, I am sick! I don't have any idea what is going on with my body. I can't even drive. Maybe I have a brain tumor, for God's sake! The session, though, is only a short walk from my house, so I think, *Ah, fuck it. I might not be able to drive, but I still have two legs that can carry me. Let's do this.* And off I go.

A few blocks later, I arrive at Teri's home, where the mystical Dr. J is staying. He greets me personally, and I feel warmth oozing out of his pores. He has kind hands, intense brown eyes, and a deep voice. His accent is strong enough that I have to pay attention quite closely to every word he says lest I miss any key pieces of wisdom.

"Let's talk about goals for a moment, Barbara," he starts. "Goals are the keys in making a happy life. Without a direction, we will just swirl around and never get anywhere," he says. He's speaking my language. I'm a "get shit done" kind of girl. I can do this! I am extremely good at setting goals and achieving them. That is my main coping strategy and how I have survived for much of my life. Controlling the world around me serves me well, and my ability to manifest the next job or raise or home is a point of pride.

"Do you know the difference between the conscious and subconscious mind?" he continues. "To make a happy life we must have goals, but those goals must not be created by our conscious minds. It is the process of connecting to our subconscious mind that will lead us to inner peace and happiness." Unfortunately, none of my goal-setting skills are what I need right now. External pursuits won't cut it. What I need is patience, awareness, self-love, and trust. Lots of trust. He writes notes in the notebook I'd grabbed from my daughter's school supplies and tells me to draw a picture of a horse-drawn carriage.

"Quite good," he says. "Goals are the horses that carry the carriage." *All right,* I think. *That seems reasonable.* Maybe this whole thing is going to be okay.

Then Dr. J throws me for a loop. "Now, we meditate," he says. Ugh! Sitting in one place has never been my strong suit, and my body responds accordingly. My eyes want to open, my spine slouches, and my nose itches. It is incredibly difficult to sit there, facing a master of meditation who is very happy in his guru pose.

I feel like we sit there for ten years—seriously. My mind wanders. I think about what the birds are talking about outside, what I am going to have for dinner, what Mr. Mister might be doing at this moment. I feel like I am in prison, forced to sit still and not think, which of course, is all I can think about.

As our session is ending, and I am not sure I've gotten anything out of this process at all, Dr. J gives me a fourteen-day assignment that includes breath-based meditation and a journal exercise. That's easy enough since I already have a journal practice. He says that the purpose of my homework is "to move from the conscious mind to the subconscious mind," where I will find and be able to identify my truest, most authentic goals.

I thank Dr. J and head on my way, feeling calm and even a little bit hopeful that this could help me find a path out of my chaotic life.

Since I was a kid, my logical (conscious) mind has always been in charge. I love learning and being challenged and am usually the one to take charge in group situations, so we can achieve our goals faster. Society rewards me for this behavior, and it is the role I am most comfortable playing. Dr. J believes my suffering is caused by my conscious mind and that the only way beyond my suffering is to get beyond my conscious mind. And that, for whatever reason, makes a lot of sense to my logical mind.

As Dr. J instructed, every day I sit comfortably in my bed and look at my Quan Yin statue, the Buddhist goddess of compassion, mercy, and healing. I sit with my spine straight up and down, and breathe naturally in the pattern Dr. J gave me, which gives my conscious brain a task to focus on:

- Breathe in and breathe out once
- Breathe in and breathe out twice (counting each breath)
- Breathe in and breathe out three times (counting each breath)
- Breathe in and breathe out four times (counting each breath)
- Breathe in and breathe out five times (counting each breath)
- Breathe in and breathe out four times (counting each breath)
- Breathe in and breathe out three times (counting each breath)
- Breathe in and breathe out two times (counting each breath)
- Breathe in and breathe out one time

The experience is like climbing a hill and then walking back down the other side. After a few days of this practice, I can feel a shift in my gut after a few breaths—like a gear that literally goes *clunk* inside my stomach as it moves into the right place. I feel energy move from my head down into my heart and then my solar plexus, the space just below my ribs and diaphragm. Even though I resist the idea of having anything other than my brain in charge, this shift feels good. I feel centered and self-contained, as though I've returned from the chaos of my life into a calm and collected body and mind.

For the first three or four days, I open my journal after each meditation session and write the answer to the question,

"What do I want?" I like taking action, so my answers are always tangible things: a bigger house, a loving relationship, my debt paid off, more income. But that doesn't seem to fit into the deeper spiritual context Dr. J was asking me to uncover.

From days five to fourteen, I write the answer to the question, "What do I need?" My answers here are often "blank, blah, nothing is coming," which is really frustrating. My conscious mind pipes in: *I'm doing this wrong. This will never work. WTF?* Eventually though, after a few days, words actually begin to come, and my pages start to fill. Now, as I put my pen to the paper, I write whatever comes to my mind. No filtering. I write until I feel finished and then turn the page. Dr. J says it is important not to read any of my entries just yet.

On the fourteenth day, I begin to meditate.

"You need to spend a year without a man."

My eyes fly open, springing me out of my deep state. The voice is so clear, it is as if someone is in the same room talking to me. I look around to be certain no one else is there. There is a big difference between thinking a thought and receiving information. In this moment, I receive the message.

Just as abruptly, other voices, echoes of conversations with family members, begin to ring in my ears.

"Barbara, you change men like most people change underwear."

"I just buy an extra gift in a large for whatever man Barb brings to Christmas."

"I am telling you, Barb, you go through men like water through a sieve."

The idea of being without a man suddenly makes perfect sense to me, an about-to-be-twice-divorced woman in my late forties. I have spent a lifetime seeking my purpose, seeking wholeness, seeking independence, but always, always, always seeking a man to complete me. *Maybe I do need a year without a man,* I wonder.

On day fifteen, I meditate and then go back to read through the two weeks of notes with a highlighter in hand. This step is to highlight only those things that strike me. No thinking, no analysis, no consideration. I just highlight the words and ideas that resonate with me. The final step is to take three pieces of paper, review the highlighted items, and write my objectives for the next three years, one year on each piece of paper. Even as I write this now, the process seems preposterous. How could a goal that isn't created from a specific identified need, established after analysis and consideration, be valid? My thinking mind is going crazy. However, the results are striking. As I review the pages, it is clear that what I need is peace of mind, rest, and then I see it—clear as day in my own handwriting: "I need . . . a year without a man."

That is it! That is it! The idea of taking my love life, the pursuit of all pursuits for me, and setting it aside is like a parting of the seas. I have spent a lifetime working on creating a relationship with a man, improving a relationship, fixing a relationship, or finding a relationship. What would it be like to just set that need aside? What would it be like to finally face the terrorizing fear I might feel without a man in my life? Would I survive? Could I survive? Somehow, at the same time, the answer is so clear. So clear that there is no internal discussion, no real thought of not doing it. It isn't even an idea. It is the truth.

It isn't a goal that I will force into existence. This is not a creation of my goal-oriented mind. This clarity has been dropped into my being. And for the first time in a long time (maybe ever), I am listening. *What a relief!* In that moment, I realize I can set aside the stress of my obsession with Mr. Mister. I will spend one year without a man in my life. I will spend a year focused on my own growth and remove men from the equation completely. And that is when it hits me: If I hadn't gotten sick, I wouldn't have had the break from work to do the meditation and journaling assignment.

I am *so* excited to share this revelation with Gayle. I wake up the next morning feeling clear, connected, and grounded for the first time since my fainting spells began—and interestingly, the blackouts never return. The medical experts had theorized that they could be from a combination of dehydration, alcohol, migraine medication, and stress. None of them knew for sure.

Gayle and I take a walk along the creek-side path in the morning. As we take in the springtime air and blooming trees around us, I recount my process of meditation to her. I tell her about the writing, review, awareness, goal setting, and the decision I have made. "I am going to remove men from my focus for the next twelve months. No dating. No searching. No obsessing. No Mr. Mister. I am going to focus on myself and what I need to do to stand on my own. I'm going to do a year without a man," I conclude.

Gayle is quiet, which is new. She listens intently and then says something I am very much not expecting.

"I will do it with you."

"What?" I can't believe what I'm hearing. "Are you kidding?" I ask.

"No," she replies. "I will do it with you. We will do it together. The reality is I *need* to do it with you. And I do. I so very much do. I need to be with you. You have become my lifeline, and I have never been without a man. How could I possibly try that alone? I couldn't. And knowing me, I wouldn't."

Gayle

I have been so lost in the romantic fantasy of being with Mr. Married in the life I've created in my mind that I've been oblivious to how unavailable he is. I desperately want a future with him, and I never planned on being alone. I never thought I would be in this situation. When I got married, it was for life. I thought Greg and I were soulmates, yet here I am twenty-two years later, deeply in love with another man.

For months we've found excuses to meet on the slippery slope of an emotional affair. I see him as a man who would provide me with safety, security, and stability. In my mind, he would make me his priority. I am so attracted to him that I feel it on a cellular level, so deep inside my heart that it actually hurts. I fantasize about being with him on a beach, in his arms, relaxing and watching the waves crash and the sunset, knowing that later we would be making love by a fire or some other romantic setting.

It is all a big fucking lie.

Barb's revelation is as true for me as it was for her. Somewhere deep down inside, I know this is my path out of suffering.

9

———

Strategy on the Deck

Gayle

In truth, our affairs have been our drugs. We are as obsessed with the idea of a happily ever after as an addict is to their drug of choice. When I describe addiction to others, I say it is when you need something on the outside of you to fulfill some perceived thing inside of you—whether it's food or chocolate, or sex, or men, or alcohol, or sports. I remember saying to Mr. Married once, "Oh, you're like a drug to me." I didn't mean it in a healthy way. I was hooked on the dopamine rush that I would get every time I met him for lunch, received a "Good morning, beautiful" text, or he snuck over to my house with Asian takeout.

Barb's obsession is just as extreme—the high she gets when texting Mr. Mister or when having phone sex or when they are traveling feels so good, but the crash afterward brings a low like nothing else.

So like addicts, if we are going to quit, if we are going to go cold turkey, we need support. And a lot of it.

Barb's deck is our preparation station for our yearlong journey of self-discovery, self-reliance, and independence. Oddly enough, there is no fear present for me: It feels more like a relief.

We proceed to tell our families and friends about our decision to live a full year without men. Everyone is supportive. Ironically, Greg suggests we have one last night together. He takes me to dinner and gives me a card in which he wrote: "I was somewhat surprised by your announcement, but with what I know you want to achieve for yourself, I fully respect your decision. Congratulations! You are incredible." After we eat, we get a hotel room where we have sex for the last time. I cry. Nothing about it feels good. It really is time to move on.

Barb

We are leaving familiar ground and embarking on a journey into the unknown. With my corporate leadership background and Gayle's student-oriented mind and mediation skills, we get to work on a transition plan.

I had the good fortune to work with William Bridges, whose Bridges Transition Model helped me with change management in business, so I am confident it will do so again now. Bridges' work describes the psychological reorientation we will go through with any change: ending, neutral zone, and new beginning. In our case, the ending phase is our old identity of a woman looking for a man. We are leaving the core belief that we need men in our lives to be complete and to achieve happiness.

The neutral zone is the time and space between the old and new worlds that feels uncomfortable and uncertain. Bridges describes it as the first night in a new house where you can't find the light switch in the dark. It's Linus when his blanket is in the dryer. The year without a man is our neutral zone, our period of committing to doing the scariest thing either of us can think of: being alone. There will be no partners, no sex, no dating, no calls, no searching, no effort put into connecting or flirting or attracting. This is why we need support.

We will be one another's primary support person. If the toilet breaks, if we are sick, if we feel scared, we will rely on one another. If we need a "date" for a social event or holiday or Valentine's Day, we will be there for one another. If we need a reality check, we will be there. We will be the equivalent of one another's sponsor—the mirror, the listener, the teller of truths.

This feels like a big fucking deal, and we know we will need a host of support systems to get us through. So we turn to our tried-and-true world of self-help and therapy—it's time we put our knowledge into practice in the deepest of places. Certainly, spiritual teachers and experts will provide the accountability and guidance we need to transform during this radical journey.

All this support and our commitment to twelve months without men should set us up for a new beginning. Bridges says a new beginning is when new understanding, values, and attitudes appear, along with a fresh identity.

Gayle

As part of my second master's program, I was introduced to the work of Dr. David Nylund, a professor of social work and an expert on narrative therapy. Narrative therapy is based on the idea that we are multi-storied beings and specifically addresses the stories we have developed about ourselves and our lives. We often get stuck on a single story about our deficits or problems that we internalize as part of who we are.

Narrative therapy helps us externalize our stories (seeing problems, beliefs, and emotions as their own characters, separate from who we are) and rewrite them. A narrative therapist uses curiosity about alternative stories to help us see what else is possible. Barb and I are both drawn to this approach and want to integrate it into our year. We need to get to know ourselves apart from our stories about who we are.

"I think we should go see Dr. David to help us deal with our fucked-up affairs," I suggest. Barb agrees, and we make an appointment to see him the following week.

Dr. David is not what you would expect when you meet a therapist. He comes across more like a rockstar with silver earrings and rings on his fingers. He has a gift for listening to stories and pulling out the underlying beliefs and social or cultural narratives hidden within them. Much of what we think, Dr. David teaches us, are actually thoughts we built based on our experience and culture. He is brilliant at helping us recognize and externalize our emotions and the stories we have built around and in response to them. We then can see emotions and social constructs as separate entities, as if they are sitting in the chair next to us. Dr. David's work often has us conversing with a particular feeling. He asks questions such as, "What would fear want you to know about this situation?" and "How has anger stopped you from moving forward in this situation?" We love him.

Dr. David also works frequently with members of the LGBTQ community, so it isn't a big surprise that he initially thinks we are a couple. "So, how long have the two of you been together?" he asks during that first meeting. We look at each other laughing and quickly explain that we are just friends who are both struggling with similar romantic obsessions.

Our Dr. David sessions are two hours long once a month—an hour for each of us. One of us shares first, and the other acts as a scribe. After an hour, we switch. Dr. David begins to help us understand and shift the underlying beliefs that are driving our emotional reactions to our lives. As part of our year, Dr. David often summarizes our work in letters that reflect our challenges, new awareness, and our progress.

This year is our laboratory to learn, heal, grow, understand, dialogue, and theorize about what is actually happening. We both have a lot (literally decades) of therapy under our belts and know that professional help is critical to move through a man-free year as healthfully as possible. While Dr. David helps us see other possibilities, Joan, a psychotherapist, helps us dig into our patterns and past to heal wounds and behaviors. I have been seeing Joan for a decade, and after meeting her, Barb says that Joan is like the mother everyone wishes they had. Her experience, wisdom, and depth of spirit set the tone for and direct our sessions.

We also decide we will each work with a trigger point therapist Barb has been seeing for years, Javier. He brings both the ability to work through physical issues and a deep, wild wisdom about the intricacies of relational dynamics. We know that our bodies carry stress in physical ways and bodywork helps release that energy. Bodywork also provides regular, healthy physical touch, which will be crucial for the next twelve months.

Not only does Javier make connections between the body and mind, but he is also a spiritual teacher. He sees who we truly are and reminds us of that. He keeps us laughing as he loves to tell terrible jokes as a distraction from the pain his work can bring. In one of my early sessions with him, he tells me, "You are just coming into your voice, but you want validation because you've felt invisible for so long. You have no boundaries and overshare. Use discernment about who you share yourself with."

That's the kind of insight he offers as he works at the deepest level on muscles and tendons to release physical and emotional holding patterns. Barb and I agree to pay attention to the body-mind connection, taking a whole systems approach to the upcoming year by incorporating massage, yoga, walking, and meditation throughout the year. We will attend workshops on anything relating to personal growth and relationships. We also agree that we need to include some fun escapes to help get us through—Italy perhaps or a warm weekend in Mexico.

Barb

To make sure we leave no stone unturned, we even decide to try some really weird shit—channelers, psychics, and astrologers. Judith, an enlightened spiritual mentor who communicates with non-physical beings, helps with energy healing and clearing. Pat is an intuitive who offers insight and reassurance of our path. Donna works on our astrological charts as a means of offering insights from yet another perspective. We also spend time with Dr. J, the one who launched us on this path, when he is in the States. His mysticism helps us stay deeply connected with our subconscious brain, which is always seeking healing, and with the unknown as we grow.

We have our team. These are our people. We have faced

the truth: At the hands of our addiction and obsession, our lives have become unmanageable, and now is the time to face our deepest inner suffering head-on.

We agree to document the year with daily journaling. We also decide to read. A lot. We start with *When Things Fall Apart* by Pema Chödrön and *If the Buddha Dated* by Charlotte Kasl. When I first read *If the Buddha Dated*, it guides me to look at multiple levels of what I want or feel is important in a relationship. I love self-help exercises like this, so I sit down with my journal and write all my desires, including characteristics I wanted in a man, and rank them: intelligence, creative balance, integrity, stands up to me in a supportive way, physically strong, beautiful to my eyes, doesn't smoke, doesn't drink too much, wants/works toward security. . . .

After I finish writing three pages, I go into the kitchen to get some water and it hits me. *Availability!* I hadn't even written down the most important characteristic. I reopen my journal and scrawl across the top of the page: *Available—Emotionally and Legally!*

We don't feel brave or frightened; we feel certain and clear. We are going to face everything we have been hiding from for our entire lives. Our unconscious suffering will no longer be under the surface, directing our choices; it is coming out of the dark and into the light. If we can make it through this year, the rest of our lives and our relationships will be forever different. We are in our late forties, and it is like we are standing at the open door of the skydiving plane 13,500 feet in the air. As the Zen saying goes, "Leap and the net will appear"—and so we do.

As I contemplate the brave adventure ahead, Mary Oliver's

poem "The Journey" comes to mind. My favorite way to experience this poem is to hear David Whyte, who has a deep British accent tinged with Irish influence, read it aloud. He often repeats a line as if he knows it is the one line you most need to hear. So Gayle and I sit on the outdoor sofa, under the twinkling string of lights that hang from the pergola over my back deck. We face each other as we begin our journey and listen to David Whyte remind us of Mary Oliver's words.

Inspired, we set a start date: June 1, just one week away. We have some difficult prep work to do, including taking a monthlong break from alcohol and having uncomfortable conversations with the men we are obsessed with. Nonetheless, we are excited and committed. The next 365 days will be difficult, but something deep down tells us profound gifts lay waiting just down this road.

The night before we begin, I write a letter to myself:

Dearest Barb:

You are about to embark on your own personal journey. It is a journey only you can take, one that you have prepared a lifetime for. You have all you need—truly. It may not feel that way, but you do. Be open, be free, feel it all. It is a wild adventure, so set your wildness free.

It is time to clear your mind, clear your heart, and clear your body. Be kind and loving to yourself. It is time to save your own life rather than trying to save everyone else's. Act in loving ways to others, but don't do that at the expense of loving-kindness to yourself. You are the most precious one and only you can protect that.

Surround yourself with likeminded individuals—get the help you need. Be open to the experience, not tied to any outcome. Play, enjoy, experience, love with your whole heart. Live on the edge of tears—open, graceful, vulnerable—feel it all. The whole world is yours in this moment. You were born for this time. Be in it all the way.

I trust you. I trust the Universe. I trust others.

"Leap and the net will appear."

SUMMER

There will be times when standing alone feels too hard, too scary, and we'll doubt our ability to make our way through the uncertainty. Someone, somewhere, will say, "Don't do it. You don't have what it takes to survive the wilderness." This is when you reach deep into your wild heart and remind yourself, I am the wilderness.

—Brené Brown

We start our experiment at the beginning of summer. Although we are both on the path to being "alone," we have no idea how hard solo life will be or what good will come of it. But we are ready, and we are committed. Our relationships have been fucked up for far too long. We need to write new stories.

10

—

Day One, June 1, 2010

Barb

Last night, I had a little talk with Jesus—which is odd because he's not someone I usually talk to. I asked him to watch over me, and he said he would. He said it was okay that I didn't spend much time with him over the years. He still cared and had been watching over things. Feeling hopeful, I slept with a confidence about the journey ahead.

I awake on Day One feeling nervous (not scared) but anxious, like I'm not sure what to do. So I sit and meditate with my statue of Quan Yin. This always helps to calm me. And so, it begins, one year for me—364 days to go. I don't carry religion with me as a primary tool in my daily life, but I feel grateful that my faith in this decision and our support system is unwavering. *Finally,* I think, *my life will be in my hands. I get ready for the workday and head into the office.*

"How about lunch?" Mr. Mister peeks his head around the corner as he has a hundred times before.

"Sure" is my quick reply. Lunch is the way we get out of the office to have uninterrupted discussions about our work. We are really good at compartmentalizing, and we have convinced ourselves that our personal relationship never interferes with our professional one. We are the perfect team because he has vision, I am great at execution, and we hold each other in high regard professionally. I admit that I sometimes catch myself staring deeply into his blue eyes and that I occasionally let my mind wander into fantasy, but not today. Today my focus is on myself.

Our lunch is like any other working lunch. On this particular day, we are figuring out the logistics of an upcoming acquisition. He is describing how he sees the product integration, and I am working out the organizational strategy. I feel separate from him for the first time in a long time. The adrenaline of being alone with him is remarkably absent. I am committed to a new path and feel secure about it. I say nothing about my decision until we pull back into the parking lot at work.

I turn to him and calmly say, "I have decided to spend a year without a man."

"What?" he asks. "What does that mean?"

"What that means," I reply, "is I am taking everything about men, the looking, the trying to understand, the seeking, the whole topic of a relationship off the table for one year. I am no longer willing to live the life that got me to where I am now. And, yes, that includes our relationship. I am not going to see you outside of work." Most conversations where we've talked about the possibility of "us" have been strained. They usually begin with some fantasy about being together and end with tension and anger about the fact that our dream isn't possible.

Today, I feel calm and empowered because, for the first time with him, I am no longer looking for him to fix my pain. I have taken responsibility for my own emotional life. When I finish talking, he simply says, "That's disappointing."

"Why is that disappointing?" I ask.

"Because I want to be with you," he replies.

As I hear these words, I feel like the top of my head is going to explode. The voice in my head starts screaming at him: *What the fuck did you just say?! After all this time and all this agony, now you say that you want to be with me? The audacity! After all the conversations about how that isn't possible, why would you say that now?* While the voice in my head continues to rage at him, my wise voice says out loud, "But that's not possible; you're not in a position to be with me."

"It's the truth," he repeats. "I want to be with you."

I repeat, "You are not in a position to be with me."

And that is it.

The truth.

Simply said, nothing to discuss, packed into one short sentence. No drama, no hysterics, nothing to argue about. We get out of the car and return to the office. I sit at my desk and realize I am okay. He no longer holds the power. I am here for myself. And I just got a taste of what wholeness could feel like.

Of course, all of that is easy to say and much, much harder to do. One day I find myself feeling strong and in charge of myself; the next day I'm really, really mad at Mr. Mister and the if/then thinking is back: *If he will only show up, then I will be okay.* I am agitated, frustrated, and again, I look to him to come and fix it—to fix me. "Fucker!" Every time I think about the situation, that's all I can say, "Fucker! You fucker!" Blame comes easily, and anger is always either bubbling over the edge or lurking just beneath the surface.

Twenty years ago, my first therapist taught me to ask my internal observer to pay attention to my thoughts, actions, and behaviors and to provide me insight. I am grateful for her presence now and what she notices going on inside me. I am still on the path, but I am pissed, pissed, pissed that I have to be. I guess that is a good thing and part of the healing. Years of therapy have helped me to recognize the wound from the early loss of my dad, but the experience I am having right now is exposing how tender that wound still is. The depth of the pain in my solar plexus feels vast and endless, like it will overwhelm my whole body.

My challenge, really, is to learn to trust myself and to become vulnerable enough to feel the pain until it heals. I am giving myself a year to figure it out, and I will have to keep turning my focus back on myself. I can't keep blaming Mr. Mister.

Our Dr. David session on Day One is the first time we've seen him since my medical crisis, the Dr. J assignment, and our decision to embark on the year without a man. After catching Dr. David up on all that had happened in the months prior, I tell him that the outcome of the Dr. J process was that I got very clear that everything in my life was secondary to this single pursuit of finding *the right man*. Every time I would see a man, I would think, *Is he the one, is he the one, is he the one?*

Dr. David asks, "Why is this important to you?"

"Because I want to live my life from the inside out," I respond.

"Have you been trying to live your life from the inside out?"

"Relationships have been sucking the life out of me, especially my relationship with Mr. Mister."

"Do you need to have a year to be able to 'go into a bar and not drink'?" he asks metaphorically.

"I really just want to live an authentic life," I reply.

"What does authentic look like to you?"

"When my inner life and my outer life are in alignment, which they are not today," I explain. "But I'm afraid that if I do this year, I'll always be alone."

"The fear tricks you to believe that if you do one year alone, you'll always be alone."

Gayle

I begin Day One not with thoughts of my ending marriage, but with the promise of a future with Mr. Married. Even though my children are home for the summer and I have loads of schoolwork to complete, there is no switch that will turn off the desire, obsessive hope, and running inner dialogue.

In the afternoon, though, when Barb and I are on our way home from the appointment with Dr. David, we feel so empowered because he sees us as capable and strong. He's on the journey with us. Dr. David and Barb both give me the strength I need to make the call to Mr. Married to say goodbye. Making this call is difficult, but necessary. We pull over at an entrance to a trailer park off the highway, and Barb steps out of the car to make a business call and give me some privacy.

It's ringing. I feel sick to my stomach. This is it. The last goodbye. For good this time. I already know it will be one of the hardest, yet probably one of the most freeing conversations I'll ever have. I have to do it. I made a commitment to myself to a life of authenticity and integrity. I had wanted one last fix and had arranged to meet Mr. Married in person later that day to say goodbye, but Dr. David helped me realize that would not be healthy. Canceling my planned rendezvous to feel that one last embrace, to have him hold me as I cry, is the right thing to do, the most loving and kind thing to do for me.

"Hi," I say. "I want to let you know I am not going to be able to see you today. I need to cancel our plans. You know I love you. But I'm calling to say goodbye for good."

Silence.

"Are you there?" He assures me he is, and I continue. "This is hard for me to say, and I wanted to see you in person so you could comfort me and I could look into your eyes one last time." I explain the plan for a year without a man.

"It's the right thing to do for both of us," he says.

I tell him I can't be his friend. "I need to have a clear mind. My obsessive thoughts about you are making that impossible. They've been keeping me chained."

"Look," he says. "I wish I could be there to hold you now. The truth is I have never been as open and honest with anyone in my life as I've been with you. But I understand. Thanks for letting me into your world, Gayle."

"You aren't the cause of my decision to do this," I tell him in an effort to maintain some of my power. "This will be a year of clarity, a year of having me as my primary relationship. If ever you and I can have the relationship we dream of, this is the only way it can happen. I am not doing this for you. I am doing this for me."

"I understand," he replies. "You deserve better. I trust and have faith that whatever is meant to happen will happen." As he talks, a combination of sadness, fear, nervousness, empowerment, and clarity washes over me.

I go on. "I have never felt the level of attraction for anyone as I do with you. I hope a year from now you will be in a position to be with me. But in the meantime, I would really like to avoid seeing you, if at all possible. It's just too hard."

"In that case," he tells me, "you should probably not go to the hospital fundraising event this weekend." We were both planning to attend it in just a few days. That's when I begin to cry as the reality of not being with him for a whole year finally hits me and fear takes the front seat. "I love you," I say. "Goodbye."

"It's going to be okay," he says. "You are going to be okay. I love you. Bye, Gayle."

Barb gets back in the car, and a jumble of emotions swirls inside me again. I did it! I just set down the bottle! I am excited about the possibilities that lie ahead. I'm moving forward. I'll be free from the pursuit of finding a man and the belief that I need to have a man in my life to be okay.

The next morning, however, I wake up again with thoughts of Mr. Married. I am in my house alone, yet I dreamed that one day after his divorce, he would move in with me. I am committed to not contacting him, so every time I want to reach out, I allow myself to write a text or email. Instead of sending it to Mr. Married though, I send it to Barb. The practice helps me face the obsessive thoughts. These letters and texts usually begin with "Hi Barb. This is me not texting him . . ." and are followed by long, emotional outbursts:

> I did not plan this. I NEVER thought that I would be in
> this situation. When I married it was for life. I thought Greg

and I were soulmates. Now here I am twenty-three years later, and I am deeply in love with another man. A man who defies the boundaries of what I thought love was. A man who is a perfect fit for me and what I want for myself and my future life.   A man I am so attracted to that I feel it on a cellular level, so deep inside, so in my heart that it actually hurts. A man I trust who provides me with safety, security, and stability. A man with the same values as me. A man who I respect beyond all others. A man who I know would never cheat on me or abuse alcohol. A man who would love me the way I deserve to be loved. A man who understands and feels the same way about me. A man who would be willing to make this relationship with me a priority. A strong man who is not afraid to share his fears with me, his past traumas and nightmares, his flaws, his tears. A man who takes care of himself and works on being healthy. A man who would take care of me too. Mr. Married, that man is you. I LOVE YOU. I want you. I want to have a future with you. I am starting to believe that in a few years, these dreams could possibly manifest into reality. See you in my dreams again tonight. I love you. I know this much is true.

Over the course of the year, I will write pages and pages of the same. In one of the letters I write: "I understand that we aren't able to give our relationship the attention it needs right now, but we still need to nurture it in ways that we can, when we can. You wouldn't be the man that I love if you were not doing what you are doing at home at this very moment."

Barb and I read that line together and chime in simultaneously, "That's fucked up." We find ourselves saying this a lot because, well, it really is.

Barb

Thankfully, the Dr. David sessions are intense, insightful, and intimate, and we are eager students. After our sessions, we find a booth in a nearby restaurant and spend hours pouring over our notes in pursuit of learning, healing, and growth around the big issue—our belief that we have to have a man in our lives to feel complete and find happiness.

Shortly after our June session, we receive an email from FEAR (by way of Dr. David):

Hi Barb & Gayle,

I wanted to let you both know that I am not scared of your so-called progress. Sure, you're saying you'll go a year without a man, but are you sure you can stay on track? Remember, a year is 365 days long!!

You both have to admit that I have been quite successful in convincing you that you need men in order to be happy; that you are only complete with a man. I have persuaded you both to believe that it's too much to be alone, that you can't do it. You'll be lonely, empty, and sad. You know that you can't do this without sex and/or mind-altering substances to cope; that facing the present moment, with the multitude of thoughts, pain, and cravings is too much to handle.

Are you sure that you are not going back to your old ways? Gayle, shouldn't you listen to me? Haven't I been there for you?

Okay. . . . I will have to admit, I am a bit scared that you have recently made such so-called progress. You surprised me, and I have to respect you for it (I don't like it, though). The relationship between the two of you is very threatening to me. Why is that? You both speak so clearly lately—with so much certainty, strength, and commitment. You've surprised me. I thought I could take you for granted.

Well, I am not going away just yet. I am planning my counter-strategies. Be on the lookout.

With respect,
FEAR (and my friends GUILT, PEOPLE PLEASING, LIVING A LIFE FOR OTHERS, MALE DOMINANCE, and CRAVINGS).

When I read his email, my fingers quickly type this reply:

Dear FEAR:

As I started to read this letter from you, my heart began to race and my thoughts began to shift toward doubt and questioning. That chatter was quickly replaced with a loud "Fuck you." I don't know if that is denial or progress, but it felt good that something inside of me stood up and said, "No. Enough." You can try to work your way back into the dominant position in my psyche, and you may even succeed in some small ways, but I am connected to an old, lost part of myself that won't go down easily. Bring it on!
Barb

A few moments after I send my reply, my computer dings with a response from Gayle too. It reads:

Ditto!

11

Manless Mondays

Barb

"How's the year without a man going?" asks Hollie, the friend whose name I could not remember just a short time ago.

We are sitting in the window seat of our favorite restaurant, listening to the guitarist playing in the corner, watching passersby through the window, enjoying some great food. We've been friends for fifteen years. She is married with a large family, has an outgoing disposition, and is well known in our community from her years as an on-air personality at the local radio station.

Just this morning I'd written in my journal:

I feel like I have begun an ultramarathon with a huge hill at the very beginning. I am moving in the same direction, and my commitment is still solid, but I feel as though my limbs are made of something surprisingly heavy, and that I have to drag this extra weight with me as I run up this very steep hill. I know I need to pace myself and give myself permission to accept where I am, to not push or have angst about my speed of progress or attitude. I need to be willing, as Joseph Campbell has suggested, to get rid of the life I've planned, so as to have the life that is waiting for me. Willingness, I decide, is the key in this moment. I am choosing freedom, and that is what I will have. I feel trapped by the thoughts that have kept me in this place, and want freedom from my clinginess to others and from my insatiable need for love and energy from them. I feel like an addict who has set down her drink for the last time.

I'd also gone back through my recent journal entries to see how much time and energy I'd spent on my fucked-up relationships. It is the topic of nearly every entry. So, I've decided to take a break and go have some fun with Hollie.

"I feel like all I am doing is working and yelling at Sammy to get her homework finished. It's exhausting," I tell her. With a sigh, I add, "I'm learning a lot about myself, but there are a few things I really miss. Sometimes having a man around is just easier."

"Easier, how?" Hollie asks sincerely. "I keep thinking how nice it would be to make all of the decisions about my life without having to consider anyone else. If you want to travel, you travel. If you want to eat cereal for dinner, you eat cereal. You get to decide on the movie you want to watch. Every time. I have to admit that I'm a little jealous."

"Well, don't be too jealous," I try to assure her. "While all of those things are true, sometimes it's nice to have some help. Like with the boat, for instance. I got it in the separation, but I realize I don't actually know how to launch it without Steve's help."

"Why can't we do it, Barb?" Hollie says. "Let's take it out Monday after work. It will be another milestone. Gayle has class, but I'll meet you at your place, and we'll figure it out. We'll call it Manless Mondays. My husband can fend for the kids. We both deserve the break. Now drink up. Cheers! Here's to Manless Mondays."

I am comfortable driving the boat, putting it on the trailer, and taking it off the trailer, but I was always the first mate, never the captain. Fear has kept me from the harder tasks like backing up the trailer and launching the boat by myself. Monday will be our girls' lake day.

On Monday of that first week, I hook the boat to the back of my Chevy Tahoe, and away we go for an evening of boating and swimming. I call my grown son, Brent, to ensure we have all of the steps in the right order:

1. Get the truck and boat in position to back down the ramp.
2. Remove the straps that hold the back of the boat to the trailer.
3. Unhook the front strap that holds the front of the boat to the trailer.
4. Put the plug in the boat near the motor.
5. Turn on the bilge pump.
6. Slowly back down the ramp until the boat is clearly floating.
7. Lower the outdrive of the motor into the water.
8. Start the boat.
9. Drive it off the trailer.
10. Park the trailer.

Okay, we've got it. Confidently, we follow the steps and begin backing the boat toward the water. As the boat hits the edge of the lake, Hollie looks over at me. "Did you put the plug in?"

"Shit!" I exclaim. I slam on the brakes, pull the truck

forward, hop out, find the plug, and screw it into the base of the hull. "Wow! That was close."

Feeling a bit shaky at the near disaster, we manage to launch the boat. We pull away, and as soon as we get past the no-wake zone, I let the motor roar. We scream with delight, racing across the lake, letting the wind blow in our faces, enjoying the sun, the wind, and the sheer power of controlling the boat. We spend hours swimming and floating. We have a picnic dinner of southwestern chicken salad from the local grocery store along with a bottle of our favorite chardonnay, which we enjoy while watching the sun fall closer and closer to the horizon.

Eventually, regrettably, it is time to head back. We reach the dock, and I disembark while Hollie holds the boat steady at the dock. I back the truck down the ramp, and we guide the boat onto the trailer almost effortlessly.

"That was easy!" Hollie remarks. "Why do men always seem to struggle with this part?"

I laugh, jump into the driver's seat, and slowly begin pulling the boat up the ramp.

"Stop!" Hollie screams.

Again, I slam on the brakes. "What?"

"Raise the motor!" Another near disaster averted as I had nearly let the propeller scrape the ramp bottom, which could have destroyed it. That is the beauty of girlfriends. No judgment, just assistance.

I turn back toward the truck and see two very capable men standing near us on the boat ramp next to their sailboat. Each has a half smile as they watch us. I look up at them, smile, and say, "This will be our little secret, okay?" We all laugh as Hollie and I hop back in the truck and high-five one another. We did it! One more thing that we don't need a man for. I feel strong, capable, independent . . . and a little exhausted.

After Hollie goes home, I crawl into bed and fall into a dream: I am standing on a small raft, maybe three or four feet wide, on a dark, stormy ocean. Black clouds fill the sky, and there is no land to be seen. The waves are moving the raft up, down, and around. It is difficult to stand up but not impossible. There are two other rafts, one in front of me and one behind me. Each raft has a man standing on it, holding one of my hands. I am leaning forward to hold on to the man's hand in front of me while reaching back with my other arm to grasp the man behind me. I know that I am moving toward the man ahead of me, but I am terrified of letting go of the man behind me.

I wake with a start. That image hits me hard, taking my breath away; it tells my story perfectly. Don't let one man go before you have a new man firmly in your grasp. *No shit. Wow.* Right there, is my whole fucking life summed up in one image. I hope this year will help me stand on my own, even if it is on a dark, stormy sea.

12

—

The Lesson of Loneliness

Gayle

I have plenty to keep me occupied—classes, schoolwork, time with my children, therapy, dates with Barb. When I do have free time, I spend it on a houseboat with my close friend Mimi. If I'm not by myself, then maybe the obsessive thoughts will ease up.

Only a few weeks have passed since my last rendezvous with Mr. Married and the connection that has been sustaining me. I need to let go of my need for that connection. I'm committed to going man-free for eleven more months, and I get mad at myself whenever I allow my mind to focus on thoughts of him. I wake up at four in the morning from another obsessive dream about Mr. Married and think to myself, *Oh, Gayle. He really does have all the power.*

One day my friend Asha asks me, "What is it that is blocking you? What is holding you back?"

I don't have an answer. So I start asking myself a series of questions. *What is it that is keeping me from surrendering? Is it fear of emotional pain? Is it the uncertainty of what happens next?* Suddenly, the answer is crystal clear. It is the attachment I have to a vision of Mr. Married that I turned into the fantasy of what my life with him would be like: In my mind, he is dressed in his suit and tie. He moves toward me. He pulls me in for a hug and holds me in a warm embrace. I am flooded with a deep sense of peace, love, safety, affection, and security. It is an emotional connection that satisfies me like no other experience. He gently holds the sides of my face in his hands and kisses me. I feel a flush in my heart, which travels through the entirety of my being. The intensity of our connection is like a magical drug that takes away any and all feelings of discomfort, loneliness, or insecurity. My spirit soars in that moment, and a calming warmth washes over my heart. Love is present. I am whole. But that potent, magnetic connection exists only in the fantasy of us, not in reality—and I don't want to let go of it.

The truth is that I rarely had those feelings in real life. In reality, he rarely made time for me. It was a chore to find time together and put so much energy into our secrecy. I mostly felt depleted. Clinging, yearning, wanting. But never fully satisfied. And I am tired of that. I am no longer willing to settle for crumbs. I want the whole cake.

During a therapy session with Joan, while digging into my childhood, I finally come to understand those rare moments with Mr. Married were filling the needs of the little girl in me who wanted nothing more than to receive affection from and have an emotional connection with her dad. Mr. Married represents my dad. I made him the stand-in for what I had longed for from my dad. That's why I loved the suit, the clean-cut look, the high morals, and the responsibility he takes for his life. He doesn't do drugs or have issues with alcohol. I have been projecting my needs onto him, and he had been playing the part perfectly by doing and saying the right things on the occasions when I did see him. My psyche refuses to let him go because my inner child feels she was finally getting that core need met—even though those moments were few and far between.

With the level of stress I am under from my obsession, I need all of the help I can get. I recall my friend Teri telling me about her initial meeting with Dr. J when she was traveling to Dubai. Although she had no symptoms at the time, Dr. J informed her that there was an issue in her lower right quadrant that needed attention. She figured she would look into it when she was back in the States, but her body had another plan for her. During her flight home, she started feeling sick, and when she landed, she required emergency surgery for her appendix. I felt confident that Dr. J must be an authentic energy healer. The first time I saw him, I lay on his massage table, and he didn't even touch my skin. Yet his hands sent such healing energy into my body that it seemed to alter my cells. I left in such a state of relaxation as if my being were vibrating at an out-of-this-world frequency. I even felt a little soreness in my muscles despite having had no physical contact.

When Dr. J returns to our community, I set up several sessions with him. Initially, he has me sit upright on a cushion on the floor. He instructs me how to breathe deeply down into my solar plexus and meditate. I feel self-conscious but enter into a state of calmness and connectedness.

Next, Dr. J instructs me to draw my goals. I'm not much of an artist, but I do as I'm told. I draw a stick figure of me with lines emanating out of my heart center like a child's drawing of sun rays, with a fish rising out of water representing my evolution to a glowing healthy being as my number one goal. My second goal is two stick figures, Barb and me, beside an open book next to a movie reel. My third goal is of a pair of stick figures, one male and one female, smiling with their arms outstretched toward each other with the same beaming energy I drew in my first goal.

We remain seated on the floor as he speaks in his thick Indian accent and draws what he sees as my aura: violet light emanating from my crown, green in my heart area, red in my sacral chakra, and yellow and gold toward my legs and feet. Then he uses a black pen on white notebook paper to write out his teachings that are unique to me. First, I need to realize that my thoughts and beliefs are keeping me "like an elephant whose ankles are bound in chains." He then draws an elephant with its ankles bound in chains. Next, I need to see "thoughts which come and disturb your concentration." He explains that my restlessness and doubt will go away when I focus on my goals. "This is how you will gain clarity of mind." After that, he writes and underlines "BEWARE OF THOUGHTS OF MEN THAT DISTRACT YOU." He also tells me to avoid anger through forgiveness and "don't be with men in a friendly way." That could be hard because I naturally have a way with men—friendly and borderline flirtatious. Then he lists goals he saw for me:

1. Divorce
2. Education
3. Job
4. Partner

My homework is to use colored crayons to redraw my goals on separate pieces of paper. Being used to intense academic assignments that are not relaxing or necessarily creative,

I love how Dr. J opens up my mind, getting me out of my rigid left brain and into my creative right hemisphere.

After our session, I fall into a deep heavy sleep on the outdoor sofa on Barb's deck in the middle of the day. I know it sounds weird, but it feels like an energetic shift is occurring inside me.

13

Sometimes Things Break Down

Gayle

"Admit it, Gayle. You got exactly what you wanted," Barb says angrily. "You wanted him to know you knew about our relationship so you wouldn't be left out."

"That's not true. . . ." I start, but then I realize, it is true. I didn't want to be left out of the bubble. I saw Mr. Mister at a party and had a conversation that revealed I was aware of their relationship. I used my Gayle-force to be in on the secret.

"I trusted you, and you broke my confidence," Barb says, her voice filled with utter disgust. "If it wasn't for this year, our friendship would be over." Barb has very little tolerance for betrayal. And rightfully so.

"I am so sorry, Barb. You're right. I wish I could take it back, and I know I overstepped. What can I do to make it up to you?"

We are, once again, in our favorite spot on Barb's back deck, but this time, rather than discussing our journey together, she is angry with me.

The thought of screwing up my relationship with Barb is incredibly distressing. I feel sick inside. There is no way I can get through this year without her. My need to be "in on the secret" overrode any concern I had about the impact this could have on Barb or our relationship. So I throw out the white flag.

"This is so much harder than I had thought it would be. I don't know if I can do it without you," I say to Barb. "I'll just go back to my old life. I'll give up. I will just beg Greg to try to work things out with me. This single-woman gig is not working out, not without you."

"Don't be ridiculous," Barb says, changing her tone. "That is just fear talking. You just have to know you crossed a line, and I won't have it. I don't want to do this year with you if that is how you are going to show up."

She is right. "I take full responsibility, and I am so sorry." I realize I have so much work to do. What is not my business is really, really not my business. The secrets and vulnerability she shared with me are precious. I must protect them and earn her trust. My need to feel included could have cost me my relationship with Barb.

"Bottom line, Gayle, I am not walking away and neither are you." In that moment, Barb realizes that when I told her about the party and the conversation between Mr. Mister and me, she was terrified, terrified that he would be mad, and that's why she was so angry. "I was concerned that he would pull away from me because of it. All I could think about was that he would reject me, and that was more than I could bear," she confesses. "But that fear, as great as it was, isn't enough for me to walk away from the year or from you, Gayle."

Incredibly, Barb does not walk away from me or our friendship, which she recognizes as a new behavior. She stays and works through it with me. Thank God! We agree that we are interdependent, not codependent, and that we will keep our commitment to doing this work together and respect each other's trust.

14

———

The Blessing Moon and Synchronicity

Gayle

Barb has been gone for a week. Although she travels often for work, she took a trip to Honolulu just for herself. It's incredibly brave of her. I can't wait to hear about it. I couldn't imagine traveling all by myself. Here I am in my late forties, and I've never traveled by myself, while Barb is frequently traveling the globe on her own. I've only ever traveled with Greg and my kids. The thought of getting a flight and rental car and going to dinner alone sounds terrifying to me.

As soon as she returns, I show up at her house, and we get comfortable in our usual spots on the back deck. "I took advantage of my alone time," she tells me. "While I was there, I realized I have the ability to love myself more than a relationship can love me. I listened to myself. One night I felt like going to bed, realized it was only seven o'clock, and thought, *Who cares?* I went to bed at seven. The time alone gave me access to a new level of inner dialogue with myself than I had ever had before."

"I just can't imagine spending that much time alone," I tell her. "I think if I did, I would spend it obsessing about Mr. Married."

"I spent some time doing that." Barb laughs. "I also went through a workbook on soulmates. It had an exercise where

I asked myself a set of really helpful questions. The prompt I used was how to master my aloneness. First, I identified the challenges with mastering my aloneness where clinging to an unhealthy relationship came right to the surface. Then I had to identify the opportunities to master my aloneness. I listed the ability to love myself more than a relationship and honoring/respecting my own needs. Then I got very real about my core limiting beliefs. Deep down, I believe that 1) There is no one there for me, 2) I am unworthy/unlovable/unwanted/invisible, 3) I am responsible for others, 4) I am alone—to survive I only have myself. It was really sad to realize what my internal dialogue has been. Thankfully, the final step was to go back over the list and note which of these beliefs actually have a real basis or none at all. If I was unsure, then I had to figure out what steps to take to determine if there was a real basis for a belief.

"Every day I ran past the marina and the beautiful boats and down to the park where I could watch the surfers. One day I bought a leather-bound journal and began to write letters to Mr. Mister at the quiet beach. Letters that included everything I wanted to communicate about our relationship but would never send—although I was secretly hoping I could send them someday. Then I would go back to the hotel and have breakfast. I committed to only doing what I wanted to do when I wanted to do it. It really helped me listen to myself. I made no plans. It was so outside the normal patterns of my day-to-day life, and, to my surprise, it felt great. I had no needs to meet except my own. There was no outside pressure to do or be anything other than what I felt like doing or being in the moment."

"Did you go out to dinner alone?" I ask Barb, fascinated.

"Not much, really. I decided before I left to turn off all media. In the *Artist's Way at Work*, the authors teach the concept of media deprivation—no access to any media for a week, no Facebook, no newspaper, no television. It really helped to quiet the chatter in my mind. Honestly, I am back feeling more in touch with my true self."

"I think I recognized some truth about myself last week as well," I say. "I saw Mr. Married in town after months of not having seen him at all. Just the sight of him sent me reeling and reminded me of the depth of my obsession. I had a physical reaction when I saw him. I felt flush from my cheeks down to my chest, and I worried that my face was red. I could feel the nerves in my stomach. My heart started racing, but thankfully, I realized I had a choice. I turned and walked away before he saw me."

"That's great," Barb says.

"Yeah. It's interesting. Asha and I were talking this morning, and she asked me why I wasn't angry with him. I realized I haven't allowed myself to go there yet, but I know it is inevitable and necessary to help me fully let go of him. I keep saying to myself, *Not until after August fifteenth*, after my comprehensive exams, which I have to pass before I can move on to my internship. As if the freaking grief process is something I can schedule on a calendar. Anyway, I'm free to get good and mad then. I cannot be sidetracked. I cannot obsess over him right now. My comps are the priority. I have to focus. I'm relieved that finally something in my life is more important to me than he is."

"Hey, I forgot to tell you. I had a session with Pat while I was in Hawaii and got the recording in the mail today," Barb says. Pat is an intuitive Barb has gone to for many years for spiritual guidance, insight, and direction. Barb has told me before how uncanny Pat's gifts are.

"Oh, can we listen to it now?" I ask. Not a huge fan of technology, Pat records her sessions on cassette tapes and then mails the tapes to her clients. Barb pulls out the tape, searches in the closet for her old tape player, puts the tape in, and presses "Play." We begin to listen.

Pat's voice, lilted with a slight British accent, fills the evening sky: "Have an affair with yourself. Be elegantly selfish and do what you want to take care of yourself." We relax and gaze at an amazing full moon rising through the pine trees. Just as the moon rises, at that exact moment, Pat's voice on the recording says, "July twenty-fifth will be the Blessing Moon. . . ."

"Wait. What's today?" I ask. It is the twenty-fifth, and we are looking at the Blessing Moon that Pat is talking about, during a conversation that happened a week before, 3,000 miles away, on a tape that arrived today. What a sign! We laugh, clap, and hug at the synchronicity of it all. The world *is* a magical place that has larger forces than us at work. As the drama and noise of our dysfunctional relationships has gotten quieter and quieter, we are more and more open to receiving signs from the universe that we are on the right path. We don't have to work so hard to find the messages; they keep coming to us. And we are ready to see them. Like this Blessing Moon.

15

—

Surrender

Barb

We are three months into the year, and I find myself still writing letters that I will never send to Mr. Mister. *Is this a step backward?* We see each other every day at work. Most of the time, I can keep the separation separate, but sometimes a glance or a memory will trigger the longing as fresh and raw as if it were the first day of swearing off men. In truth, we both compartmentalize well, and, really, he is so shut down and unhappy that it doesn't seem to be a problem for him either way. Other than the brief mention of his conversation with Gayle at the party a month ago, he doesn't talk about us at all. I find myself wondering, *What do I see in him that makes me long for him?*

Later at home, after a full day of work where I have spent the entire day fighting back tears, my observer self asks a question, the same question Dr. J asked during my meditation assignment: *What do you need?*

A small voice inside says, "To be somewhere where I can just let it all out." I am becoming more familiar with this small, quiet voice inside of me, and I am becoming more willing to listen to it. That's when it occurs to me that I'm home alone, and Sammy is with her dad. No one can hear me. No one is coming over. I am safe.

How about I curl up in my big soft bed and let whatever is trying to come out, come out? I climb into my tall sleigh bed that has held me close through so much, and the tears bubble up. They are soft at first, but soon they completely consume me, flooding out like rushing water through a broken dam. I am weeping, sobbing, wailing from depths I have never touched before. Completely uninhibited, I allow myself to lose track of time. I dive deeper and deeper into the wells of despair that I have so deftly avoided. My cries come for minutes, then hours. Something in me gives up the need to know how much time has passed. Something in me is allowing everything that wants to come out to come out. I don't have specific thoughts or any real sense of what I am actually crying about. I just cry and cry and cry for as long as it takes. This is the first time that I simply allow myself to surrender to my emotions. Whatever this is, I need it. The path I am on is not one of conscious thought or intention; it is one of pure surrender, and I let it take me wherever I need to go.

At some point in the night, the weeping subsides, and slowly, I feel myself moving back into awareness of my room. I am acutely aware of the present moment, of my body, and of my bed. It feels as though I am waking up from a deep sleep. First one eye opens, slowly. Then the next. I check in with my body, wiggle my fingers and my toes to find everything is working, like a child who has fallen but suddenly realizes she is okay.

I'm still here; I didn't die. Then I chuckle at the realization of how long and hard I have been working to avoid these tears. I am laughing because that place of deep emotion isn't so bad—at all. I've been covering it up with distractions like work and men, but that vulnerable place is mine. It's my center. The place I have stayed away from for so many years has come through me like a rainstorm. A very welcome, rejuvenating rainstorm that brings things back to life.

I go to sleep that night exhausted, self-contained, and amused. How silly it now seems to have resisted that refreshing, nourishing place for so long.

The next morning as a direct result of moving all that pain out of my body, I realize that my life is about so much more than the man in it. This idea seems quite obvious on one level, but it hits me with such astonishing clarity that I am floored. *Wow. I've spent most of my life never understanding that I matter, that I am enough.* My life is *my* life, and I have the ability to create it however I choose. A man in my life will be a bonus, not the main course. It also dawns on me that the relationship with the man isn't the problem; my *attachment* to the relationship with the man is the problem. And that means the problem isn't outside of me. The problem is inside of me and, therefore, entirely under my control. I can deal with that problem because it is *mine*. I am great at dealing with problems that are mine. It's why they pay me the big bucks, in fact! I can solve this.

Then another question arises within me right away, *Okay, in that case, is life valuable without a romantic relationship?* Almost as quickly a response arises: *Of course it is, so act like it.* So I decide to do just that.

It's the end of our first season, a quarter of the way through the year, and we receive another letter from Dr. David. It helps us to see how far we've come already. His guidance and support feel nurturing, and his letters are like a gift.

Barb & Gayle:

Our last meeting was quite astounding. You both came to the session with such clarity of purpose, mindfulness, and unremitting resolve to reclaim your lives from fear (and all his friends). As I listened, I was truly captivated by and immersed in your unfolding story—a story of will, purpose, resilience, and strength—that I lost myself.

The conversation that I was privileged to experience with you two was VERY different. I was spellbound and utterly engrossed in your journey of courage, of returning back to your selves. I felt connected to your experience—realizing that all of us are trying to show up in this life; that we all have our doubts, our cravings, and our relationship to suffering.

Barb, your health scare gave you a new perspective. That experience, along with many others (therapy, working with Dr. J), got you to say, "Enough already!" You had intellectually known that your relationship with Mr. Mister wasn't good for you; that always having a man wasn't good for you—that it derails you from knowing yourself. But now you have more of a spiritual, intuitive knowing of what you need (and want) to do. When you said, "I don't need a man," you were clear, confident, and direct. Damn, I wish all the women of the world could have heard it!

Barb, do you think the Barb of our first meeting would have believed your new self? Your primary focus on men was so all-encompassing that your career and parenthood came second. And, of course, you came second. Living for others was your way. Now, yours is a life of living from the "inside out."

Gayle, you realized that your relationship with Mr. Married was also an addiction. You are now thinking about a life of authenticity. When negative, critical, self-doubting thoughts enter your mind, you counter them now by externalizing them and being more cognizant of them. And you realize you don't need to act on them. You have stayed on track.

More than ever, you are committed to self-growth: getting your degree, continuing to do personal growth activities, and inspiring others. Can you see how future clients are in for a treat with you? That they will be lucky to have you as a therapist? Your pain will be a vehicle of inspiration for others as you have and will continue to harness it for productive purposes.

Gayle, your aspirations include no romance, no sex, no flirting with men, no dating, no mind-altering substances. And so far, you're doing it in spite of the Problem's insurgency. Your purification process is working—you are detoxifying from men and other things that hold you back. Doesn't the clarity feel good? How about the awakening?

Gayle, you are no longer thinking small. You are thinking BIG. Anything is possible for you now. Surely the Problem will do its best to work its way back into your life. It will do all it can to disrupt you. What do you now know about yourself that gives you this self-confidence and bravery?

I look forward with eager anticipation to our next meeting.

Yours,
Dr. David

16

Safety Net

Barb

As luck would have it, August begins with a trip to London and Stockholm with Mr. Mister. It's odd that I don't have overwhelming feelings of obsession as we plan the trip. My recent realizations and commitment to being without a man have given me a sense of freedom from the anticipation of being alone together. Our normal routine would be to get in the car to drive to the airport and hold hands for the three-hour ride to San Francisco. Then, we'd park the car and make out like teenagers until we had to rush to catch the flight.

This time, however, as we drive, we talk freely. It is open, kind, and supportive. There is no anticipation of an impending make-out session. He is interested in how I am doing, and I am interested in what is happening for him. He shares with me that he's started therapy and that it is helping him get clarity on his life. He lets me know that when I told him about the year without a man, he saw that as his timeline to figure out how he could be with me. His comment gives me a sense of hope. However, because of the insights gained in my first season without men, I recognize that a sense of hope for a future together is exactly the problem. As Dr. David says, "Hope is a vehicle for suffering; you can't completely let the thought of Mr. Mister go."

My inner voice takes over, *Stupid . . . how could you?* But then I realize that the same old pattern is trying to pull me back into its web. So I pivot, reminding myself of who I am and who I want to be. I'm learning how to live without the safety net of a man so I can be free.

The boundary of the year took the possibility of romance and sex off the table. It created space for the two of us to be together and be present with one another on this trip. I feel calm and relaxed, and the shame that I would normally feel in these moments is not there. The trip is successful on many levels—business goes well, we travel well together, and this time, lust, obsession, and desire do not hold us captive.

Gayle

I saw the movie *Eat, Pray, Love* today. I am Elizabeth Gilbert before she meets healthy love. I am her in the sense that I have had a "letting go and letting God" shift. I can feel obsession loosening its grip on me in some ways. Although nearly constant thoughts of what was, what ifs, desires, hopes, and dreams still burden me, I am not acting on them. At all. I am beginning to actually follow my inner guidance, my higher power.

A few months ago, I was sending Barb "this is me not texting him" messages almost daily. Now when anxiety rises inside of me along with the desire to reach out to Mr. Married to comfort me, I take a breath and remind myself that everything I need is already within me. I am more quickly recognizing the thought pattern that a man represents my safety net. When the voice of fear whispers, *You are going to be alone. Maybe you'll never find anyone,* sometimes I am able to see that voice as separate from me. But I still often ask Dr. David for assurance that I will have a relationship someday.

Dr. David says, "That voice, fear, is a universal voice. We all struggle with that fear." The reality is I have an inner safety net. I feel myself shifting toward an attitude of faith that I am strong enough to do this, with even a little bit of trust thrown in from time to time that I'll gain even more strength and authenticity. I tell myself that what is meant to be *will* be. I am beginning to believe that in my heart.

During a trigger point session with Javier, he reiterates what my inner guidance keeps trying to tell me. "You're much more grounded, Gayle. You are such a beautiful woman. You are special. Someday, some man is going to see that in you." With each word, it's as though he's working those truths into my cells and tissues, setting them in place. "There's a man out there who will give up his kingdom to be with you." That's the one I'm waiting for, the one I haven't met yet. For so long I've wanted to be with Mr. Married, but today I know that I want to be with the *right* man.

AUTUMN

Our pursuit of insight, learning, and growth is strong. We are on a mission to heal. The metaphor of fall, with so much change, is not lost on us, as we both seem to be spending a lot of time going inward, bundling up, and preparing for winter.

17

Invite Your Inner Guides

Barb

The loneliness comes in waves. I have a great deal of contact with Mr. Mister, and I am in love with him. I don't want anybody else. Yet I know that it's not in my best interest to let this desire rule me. In these moments, I tell myself, *Just because I'm in love with him, doesn't mean I'm meant to be with him.* I've spent so much mental and emotional time and energy on Mr. Mister that I've ignored all that's good in my life. So I am focusing on my job, bettering my relationship with my kids, and taking care of finances and business.

This journey doesn't end after the year is over. Once I'm out of the neutral zone of transition, then I face a truly new beginning. So this is not a diet; it's a lifetime practice. I need to quietly nurture the creative forces inside me that see other possibilities, other stories. Dr. David asks compelling questions this month that seem to get to the heart of the matter.

"How are you nurturing yourself? What creative forces are you tapping into? Although there's still a long way to journey, can you appreciate the present moment? You said you are proud of yourself. What are you most proud of? These qualities of letting go, self-care, and creativity are antidotes to fear, right? Are you clearer and more confident (fear doesn't govern you as much as it did in the past)?"

Questions like these are rich material for journaling. Writing first thing in the morning before my brain is fully awake allows me to dialogue with the deeper part of myself, the subconscious, as Dr. J encouraged me to do. Sometimes the questions reassure me that I am capable. At other times, I find great insight into an underlying belief or old story I cannot yet release, like my belief around what I need to feel safe or of Mr. Mister completing me, just as I expected with all the other men who preceded him (even though I never let any of them close to my heart). Now, I am practicing letting go of that idea. There are days when this notion of feeling complete without a man is so clear. And then there are days when I pine for Mr. Mister badly.

In these quiet days leading toward winter, when I feel lost, sad, and lonely, I want Mr. Mister to come to my aid. I want him to ride up on a white horse and whisk me away to a happier place, to the place where my heart has someone to focus on, where I am fueled by my connection with him. I know this place would take the edge off, but I also know it would lead me right back to where I started—a dysfunctional relationship. And I am not willing to go back there.

One morning while feeling this familiar pull, I decide to ask my older, wiser self what to do with this yearning. As quickly as I write down the question, these words arise in response: "He is not asking you for anything, so what is the question?" *Of course!*

Sitting in my bedroom, my mind is imagining a future time when Mr. Mister has taken the steps to be with me and stands before me asking for me to join him. The problem with this fantasy? He's not doing any of that! The time I have spent using my imagination to create this dramatic and beautiful story and the happiness that I have projected onto that one and only dream are tremendous. I have spent months lost in my imaginary world, giving all my power away to a man who isn't asking me to do so. He isn't actually asking me for anything. He isn't asking me on a date, he isn't asking for my opinion, he isn't asking me for a thing, *fucker!* Yet here I sit, investing all my current and future happiness in him. I've heard it said that "Worry is a senseless use of the imagination." *Well, shit! What a waste of time and energy.* Realizing this makes me feel angry, aware, and empowered. And that is very interesting.

Gayle

One cool, fall morning I awaken with the desire to capture where I'm at emotionally right now. I grab my laptop and start typing. The words come easily. Despair and loss. I am not yet feeling like the empowered, take-no-prisoners woman I had hoped to be by now. I guess I thought it would be easier a few months in. It is not. I can't help but look back at how naively I agreed to a year without a man. I am reluctant to admit that on some level, I still believe that Mr. Married and I will be together, and I will get to stay in my familiar role of wife and mother. Once this year is over, I will have my dream relationship with him. This illusion prevents me from feeling my loneliness. My psychotherapist, Joan, is teaching me the difference between loneliness and being alone. The former is experienced when you are missing another person, and the latter is the act of physically being apart from others.

Even though it was my decision to break off our relationship, it still hurts to realize Mr. Married is not trying to be with me. I used to believe his marriage was a lie, and now I realize our relationship was the lie. His relationship with his wife is actually happening. He has made his choice. He has chosen to remain a married man in every way. And he has chosen not to be with me. The one he claimed to love. The one he called Sweetheart. The one woman who, he said, would have made his dreams, our dreams, come true. Fucker! I had believed his words. Now I see that those dreams never really existed, except in my head. This wasn't the first time I was in this place. I'd spent the early years of my marriage imagining how my life with Greg would be and believing those fantasies would come true. They never did.

My heart is broken, and my eyes are open. Now I am awake. The secondary position of being the "other woman" is not where I belong. I don't want my story to be of a woman who has an affair with a married man—that's not who I am. I want a man who wants me and chooses me as his number one.

With each day that passes, the dream of being with him slowly moves further away from me. His wife has settled in the front seat beside him, not me. The dream is getting smaller in my rearview mirror. We are no longer on this path together. I'm on the road alone, and, gratefully, my mind is getting clear. Eventually, it dawns on me that I have actually been alone for a very long time. For more than a decade, I'd been missing true connection with Greg. We hadn't experienced one-on-one time, meaningful conversations, or openness about our emotions, pressures, and struggles. The only time we spent together was with our kids, and for him, even that rarely took precedence over golf, fishing, or partying.

As often happens when I'm writing, a higher, more

grounded part of me bursts through in my journaling, reminding me of the present moment, my progress, clarity, and confidence. I am accepting the things I cannot change and am changing the things I can.

I can do this.

I feel empowered.

I am choosing to head in the direction of an open, honest, loving, passionate relationship. It is my choice, the only one I can control. I choose love. I choose truth. My hands grip the wheel, and the journey on the road ahead looks promising. The view is beautiful and real. I can see it clearly now.

Barb

The drive to Joan's house is therapy in itself. Something magical happens as I turn up the road, drive past horses and then her pond, and park under the wisteria. A giant Chinese temple gong is stationed right at the center of her beautifully landscaped garden. Angel statues and a lovely statue of Quan Yin line the winding path to her door. Joan, a small, mature woman with a calm, wise demeanor, opens the door to her home office. I appreciate her tenderness, and I realize how much I need it. Her loving-kindness toward me constantly reminds me to love myself through this transition.

With each session, I gather more insights around how I give my power away and how I try to gain control. For all my life, I've used my will to create a better future—salaries, promotions, jobs, properties—without first checking in with myself to understand if it is something that I truly want. When things don't work out, I tend to blame others for my pain. One of the greatest gifts Joan gives me is the quote, "In a moment of grace, all karmic debt is released." That saying is my savior. When I realize a truth deep down and see the situation clearly, in that aha moment, all the baggage associated with it that I've been carrying around is immediately released. Those moments set me free.

I am beginning to feel self-contained more of the time. No longer heavy-hearted because of what I lack, I begin to see myself as the perfect, whole, and complete Barb I profess to be. Balance is restored, and those moments of feeling lost, scared, or desperate for Mr. Mister arise less frequently. My life is full—two kids, satisfying work, financial success, deepening friendships—I am able to survive and even sometimes thrive without a man.

In another session with Joan, she talks to me about choices. Mr. Mister is still frequently the topic of our sessions. Although my life has become much healthier and I spend a lot more time living from the inside out, I still want a life with him. I see my connection with him as something other-worldly, unlike the kind of relationships mere mortals have. I feel like we have spent past lives trying to resolve our conflicts, and I am convinced that this life is the one where we will do just that.

Joan asks me about the reality of the situation: "Is he asking you for anything?" The very same question I'd written in my journal! "Is he asking you for a relationship? Is he in a position to have a relationship with you?"

To each of these, I am forced to respond with a resounding "No."

"Why do you continue to hold on to the idea of him, when he isn't asking you for anything?" she asks.

Joan is great at focusing on what is. She is teaching me the Buddhist philosophy of suffering: suffering is caused when you want something other than what is. In these moments, that concept is a lifesaver. I have spent most of my life imagining, wishing, and working toward a vision. Very little of my life has been about standing in the *now*, in the *what is*.

Each time Joan asks another question, I sense a little imaginary string over my left shoulder, like a gnat that keeps buzzing around me. I can't really get my mind to focus on it, but I know it is there. My attempts to swat it away or ignore it go unheeded. It may not have even registered in my psyche on most days, but on this day, it does. Finally, hesitantly, I say to Joan, "There is this imaginary string I keep seeing over my left shoulder. It is an image I can't shake."

"What happens if you pull on it?" she asks.

I reach out and pull the imaginary string, and this thought hits me: *If I don't hold on to the vision of the two of us being together, then it WILL NEVER, EVER HAPPEN.*

When I share, she responds in her calm, wise, maternal voice, "That's an awful lot of power you hold. You aren't giving him much credit here." Her words stop me in my tracks.

Another image comes to my mind: I'm standing on a raised floor looking over a World War II–era warehouse, the kind where people make big, heavy, complicated machines, like cars and airplanes. It is enormous, old, and feels like it has been shut down for decades. I see the fluorescent lights coming on in this football field–sized building, section by section. One, two, three, four. I hear the big switches being flipped. *Clunk, clunk, clunk, clunk.* I see the entire building light up—that is how big my aha moment is. Immediately, memories from my childhood, teenage years, and adulthood flood in. I can see how I take control of everything and how I see myself as the one, the only one, responsible for everything. That's right! I haven't given any credit to Mr. Mister's choices, especially the choice to NOT ASK ME FOR A FUCKING THING. Regardless of what he asks or doesn't ask, wants or doesn't want, I see myself as the one who is completely responsible for the entire relationship. *Wow. That is waaaaaayyyyyyyyy too much responsibility for one person. Wow, wow, wow.* Have I really been holding on to all the responsibility for our relationship? Is our relationship something I see as mine to own? I have. And I do.

With all this awareness, I say to myself, *Fall by the wayside if you must, Mr. Mister, but I do not have to hold the weight of our relationship on my shoulders all by myself. You have to show up too. You have to do what it takes to be with me. And, if you do that, then and only then can I look at the situation and decide if I am still interested.*

A sense of freedom unlike anything I've ever known begins to wash over me. And I realize this isn't just something I do in my relationship with him. I did it with my first husband, and I did it with Steve. In fact, I take responsibility for everyone and everything in my life and try to control every aspect of all of it. It is exhausting. No wonder my body tried to opt out!

Another letter from Dr. David arrives.

Barb & Gayle:

I've been thinking of you two. I enjoy our conversations; they help me to reflect not only on your journey but my own personal voyage as a man. In particular, the kind of man I want to be in the world; what values I want to live my life by; how I want to show up in life; and what kinds of relationship skills I want to practice.

In fact, Barb, the way you have inspired Mr. Mister to move out of a stuck position and go to therapy and make progress, has inspired me.

Gayle, how's it going in exorcising Mr. Married out of your brain? It's probably one of the hardest things to do; those tentacles are powerfully built, muscular, and binding. They don't go away without a strong and persistent struggle/battle. As both of you know, craving and desire are authoritative and all-encompassing. Your struggle is one that is as old as the universe. The Buddha and monks have been overcoming desire and attachment for lifetimes. The Buddha is the only one in the history of the world who was triumphant in letting go. Gayle, are you being kind to yourself in terms of having obsessive, clinging thoughts enter your mind? Embrace them, don't push them away, and watch what happens.

Don't you think that "Gayle and Barb" is stronger than fear and attachment? How has it helped your fear of being alone? How has it helped to have an unconditional friendship with yourself? How has it helped you embrace radical acceptance—that you are exactly where you need to be, hiccups, and setbacks included? You both realize your commitment to each other is more important than a man.

Barb, wow. What happened to Mr. Mister? Complete surprise, eh? Does it make you have faith and optimism that people can change, even stuck men? Can you believe that you two were in Europe and didn't cave in to desire? It is a strong friendship, one based on mutual respect. You want to be a healthier you, a genuine, loving, authentic you. If it's in the cards, don't you think that your relationship with Mr. Mister or any other man in the future will be much healthier and stronger after this yearlong journey?

Barb, how are you being kind to yourself in terms of staying focused on self-growth and not letting a guy be primary in your life?

Are you providing a role model for your family?

It's too late to go back even if you two tried. The changes you have both made are irreversible. The fear and craving are fleeting. They have no power or truth. They're a story. Don't let the problems convince you that they're facts when they're really fiction.

All the best,
David

18

Unexpected Sex

Barb

There is a saying in Al-Anon: "Don't go to the hardware store for bread!" The notion being: They don't sell bread at the hardware store. You are the crazy one if you go there looking for bread! So, we are successfully supporting one another in *not* going to the hardware store. We are making our own bread now, together. But there is at least one area where we will need to go it alone. Sex.

Being committed to no men for four seasons is one thing, but going without sex that long is totally another. And we eventually realize we need a plan for sex. At this point, it has been months since either of us has been intimate with a man.

Remember the days when Tupperware parties were the thing? You and your friends would get together at someone's home, have wine and snacks, and look at products to keep your food fresh? Then, times changed, and women started having clothing parties where you'd do the same thing. This time, though, you'd all buy the same clothes so that you'd have to check in with each other to be sure you weren't wearing the same outfit to the next party you attended. Fortunately for us, no one we know is throwing those kinds of parties; however, Hollie decides to throw a women's only adult toy party. Now, this is *exactly* what we need. I haven't ever bought sex toys before (because of course, up until now, I've been finding my sexual gratification by moving from man to man).

Sex toys. Sex toys. *Sex toys.* Oh my God, there are so many sex toys at this party! I set aside my inner prude and invite my uninhibited self to this party. Between a man and me, I'm fine to talk about needs in the bedroom, but the thought of talking about sex in front of a group of women, some of whom are strangers, is incredibly frightening. Fortunately, I am not alone.

"Come on in and grab a cocktail, if you will excuse the pun," Hollie says enthusiastically as she throws a paper flower lei at me. "Everyone gets 'lei-ed' at this party!"

I look at the dozen women gathered in her living room. Women of all ages, shapes, sizes, and life circumstances all nervously join the conversation. I take a seat to fill out the form handed to me by Liz, our "in-home representative" who is so funny she could have been a stand-up comic.

"Ladies," she says, holding up a giant vagina pillow that looks like the most suggestive Georgia O'Keeffe painting you've ever seen. "Inside all of these layers and folds is your trip to the promised land," she says. "This little protruding piece at the top here is where you want to focus your attention. Dare we use the word? It's the clitoris. Sometimes men have trouble finding it, but I assure you each of you has one, and these lubricants and various devices are here to please you. And it!" We all giggle as she passes around the pillow for inspection.

"Nothing to be embarrassed about," Liz continues. "Plenty of us have gone through life not knowing exactly how the parts work or where to find the ones that matter the most."

She is masterful at showing us all the tools, enhancers, lotions, and potions she has for sale, and the education she gives us is game-changing. She has been married for ten years and is able to talk about the body, relationships, sex, and all the toys she is selling in a way that eliminates our concerns. We all begin to lose our inhibitions as we pass around various shapes and types of vibrators. We play with the speed settings. We feel the different textures on our hands. Very enlightening.

"Are these waterproof?" Hollie asks. "I have four teenagers! The only place I have any privacy is in the bathtub." Now we're really having fun. The evening continues with drinks, snacks, laughter, and a lot of new sex education.

From time to time, Liz says something wonderful like "Ladies, if you wish your man were a bit larger in the equipment department, might I suggest some manscaping? Nothing makes the deck look larger than some tastefully trimmed-up shrubbery." We laugh and laugh.

Gayle, lacking any inhibition, speaks up, "Do you have a large one that bends and automatically thrusts?" Liz says she does not, and that that particular device has apparently not yet been invented. At the end, Liz invites each of us to meet her in a private room to order whichever of the aforementioned items tickle our fancy. I leave with a new tool I call Mr. Purple.

One evening not too long after, I tuck myself between the sheets and close my eyes. It is just Mr. Purple and me. I hit the button and exclaim, "Holy Jesus and Mary, Mother of God!" This is new . . . this is incredible! I am not sure I will ever find a man who can please me the way Mr. Purple does.

I know Mr. Purple can't hold me as I fall asleep or comfort me when I'm feeling down, but having him makes me relax a bit. At least now I know that my sexual needs are going to be just fine.

Gayle

On the first rainy day of the year, a Sunday, I am feeling sad and nostalgic. And now there is a new uncomfortable feeling, something I haven't, until this moment, allowed myself to feel: I am mourning the end of my marriage. When Greg and I were still together, we had a tradition that he would stay home from work on the first rainy day of the year and crawl back into bed. We would order pizza, have lots of sex, and watch movies.

As I am remembering that time, a drop of water lands on my shoulder. I look up and realize the skylight in the kitchen is leaking. I pick up the house phone without thinking and call Greg—partly to tell him about the roof, and partly because I am lonely and want to feel wanted. I have a fleeting thought that he might come over to recreate our rainy-day tradition. I don't know if he meant to hit the ignore button on his cellphone, but instead, the line picks up and I can hear him talking to someone else.

"That was great, girlfriend, come back here and let's do it again." I think he is messing with me and joking, but then I hear a woman's voice and the sounds of them having sex. I can't believe it. Is this really happening? Is Greg actually having sex with another woman?! I have to call Barb. I reach over and grab my cellphone.

"Hello?" Barb answers.

"Oh my God, Barb," I whisper, "I am listening to Greg having sex." I quickly explain the mistaken call.

"Hang up the phone," she says.

"I can't. I can't. I have to know who he is with."

"Hang up the phone, Gayle. This is only going to hurt you. You guys are separated. He can have sex with anyone he chooses. Hang up. This is none of your business."

"I can't," I whisper again, frantically. "I need to know who she is—I want to know if it's that same woman as before."

"Hang up the phone, Gayle. I am not going to stay on the phone and listen to you while you listen to Greg having sex with someone else. That's fucked up."

With that, Barb hangs up. But I can't. I sit on the edge of my bed. I'm unable to move. I listen to them finish, get up, wash, and start making something to eat. *This is ridiculous,* I think to myself, but now I am enraged and self-righteous. I call his house phone. I can hear it ringing in the background.

"Hello?" he says.

"You might want to think about hanging up your cellphone!" I spew. "I just heard everything that you have been doing for the last twenty minutes. How dare you!" I scream at him. "We're still married!"

"Oh, shit," he says, and the cellphone finally disconnects.

I go on and on, yelling, crying, and hysterical. Finally, I hang up. I call Barb back.

"So, how was that for you?" Barb asks.

"I feel sick," I say.

Barb talks me off the ledge. She helps me recognize Greg has the right to be with anyone he wants to be. It still hurts me badly. And it makes me realize that our last time together really was the last time. I will never be intimate with him again. I grieve for a moment.

And then I plan.

As painful as hearing that call was, it moves me into action. I am finally ready to move forward with the divorce. I call our mediator and get online to begin the divorce process. I email the following to Greg:

Dear Greg:

It's none of my business who you have sex with. I had no idea how deep this level of heart pain hurts—to the core. I have true compassion for what it must have felt like for you when you thought I was with another man. I was wrong to think I understood how much your heart hurt. The words "I'm sorry" are not sufficient. I know that you and I are, for all intents and purposes, not husband and wife. That doesn't make it hurt any less. I was harboring a shred of hope in my heart for a possibility of you and I reconnecting, especially on a stormy Sunday.

I would like to focus on moving forward with our divorce. I filled out the online questionnaire from Divorce Helpline to get the process started. Here's the link. The next step is to call and arrange payment. Will you please do that? I'm still interested in saving our money by using mediation.

By the way, the reason I called you Sunday was to tell you that our roof is leaking. The contractor is going to come check it out.

Take care of yourself,
Gayle

He writes back within an hour:

Dear Gayle:

I'm really sorry for the way in which you found out. I also feel bad for the pain that you are feeling. I understand what it feels like, and I also realize that there are not any words that will ease what you feel. I hope that we can remain on good terms and hopefully mediate this whole process. I would like to think that we could be friends in the future and we both let go of all the old resentments and pain. I called the mediator and set up an appointment. That is the first step. I'm sure she can help us at least file. I am really, really sorry for your pain. I can only hope that you find peace and serenity in the future.

Greg

I feel sad *and* validated—this confirms that he had been having an affair long before he moved out. But I am also relieved because the truth is out—about him, about us—and he is being so agreeable about moving forward. He's willing to work with a mediator and try to maintain some goodwill between us.

I am going to have to complete myself. In the meantime, I focus my energy on my practicum where I'm seeing clients for free under supervision as part of my master's program, volunteering as a mediator at the courthouse, leading mediation trainings, and getting our house ready to go on the market. I am aware that underneath my obsessive thoughts lies the pain from the loss of my family structure and my identity as a wife and mother.

19

I Get to Choose

Gayle

I move into the holidays on my own, outside the safety of my familiar role of creating a lavish, Norman Rockwell–style feast. The first snow of the season falls on Thanksgiving Day. All three kids are home, and my parents, who live just an hour's drive away, spend the day with us. Preoccupied with the rental house I have just secured, I drive my crew over to see it. I don't have the keys yet, but we sneak into the backyard and peek through the windows. Back home, we have a simple meal and continue our tradition of sharing what we are grateful for. And I am grateful. I am grateful to be moving forward and learning how to let go. I believe that what is meant to be will be.

Barb

This Thanksgiving is the first time I will be away from my children for the holiday. My daughter will be with Steve, and my son will be with his girlfriend's family. All in all, it is a good exchange because I will have the kids for Christmas, and while I love Thanksgiving, Christmas morning with my kids in the house is my idea of mamma nirvana. I decide I will spend Thanksgiving Day with my mom and stepdad at their lakeside cabin in the Sierras, something I haven't done for many years.

I've actively avoided the inevitable drinking and subsequent arguments that occur at family gatherings.

I arrive at Mom's house around noon to an off-color comment from her husband, stepdad number two. As I walk in the door, he says, "Wow, you look great," in an overtly sexual tone while looking me up and down. My sister-in-law rolls her eyes, and I can tell the alcohol has already begun to flow. This will be an interesting day. What is it about families that keep us locked in old patterns of behavior? I have spent much of my life in therapy, trying to rewrite those patterns so I can make more conscious choices. This Thanksgiving will give me an opportunity to put my new awareness into practice.

From the outside it probably all looks fine; we cook, talk, and laugh. But with my family, no matter how merry it appears, there is always an underlying worry about someone going off the rails. It has been happening as far back as I can remember. One memory is the "Thanksgiving Day Massacre" of 1976. The whole family was gathered at the lakeside cabin for the weekend. On that fateful day, everyone sat down at the Thanksgiving table, said grace, and went around the table sharing what each of us was thankful for. Then as my sister passed me the pepper grinder, it fell perfectly into my glass of milk, splashing all over the dishes and people at one end of the table. We all laughed, with the exception of stepdad number one.

"What the hell was that, Barbara?" he started. "Pay attention to what you're doing! Look at what a mess you made!" he continued. He ranted on and on until my mother finally got him to stop. An hour or so later, everyone had either left the cabin or was locked in their respective rooms.

This year's Thanksgiving starts as family dinners often do: We sit down, say grace, then share what we are thankful for. A few minutes into the delicious meal of all my holiday favorites—candied yams, fruit salad, turkey, mashed potatoes—stepdad number two begins to talk to my brother about his life, at which point, my mother chimes in with her shrill, alcohol-induced challenges to her husband's comments. They are off and running into this year's argument about my brother's life. Stepdad number two has an opinion about everyone, and he doesn't think my brother takes his career seriously enough and will never make something meaningful out of his life.

Not one to sit in silence, I usually jump into the middle of this mess and use my psychotherapy-infused wit as a sword against the commoners. But today, as they bicker, I hear a voice—as loudly and clearly as the one that told me to spend a year without a man—say, *You don't need to be here. You get to choose. You could walk out the front door right now.*

I have always felt obligated to apologize for taking care of myself and not being a "part of the family." *Hmm. . . .* I think. *I could just get up from this table, put my dish in the sink, grab my dog and my purse, and leave? What a concept.* So I do just that. I leave without saying a word to anyone.

As I drive away, *I get to choose, I get to choose, I get to choose* runs through my head. I have taken care of myself first and done what my own body and mind need. I have chosen to leave the scene of a familiar family crime. I do it without anger, without judgment, without self-righteousness. I do it with clarity that the scene they are choosing to create is not one I desire to be in. I get to choose.

Walking away from Thanksgiving, I feel a kind of freedom that gives me permission to create my own special holiday season. I can't recall a time when I felt so full of creativity and love. My heart is open wide. I will create the most special Christmas with my children and friends. It will be magical and dramatically different.

Since that Thanksgiving moment, I no longer desire the answers to all my unanswered questions about my life. I no longer seek a clear picture of what my future is going to look like—or who will be in it with me. I simply ask for clarity in the moment. And then I listen. Sometimes answers come quietly, sometimes loudly. Sometimes answers come quickly, sometimes slowly, but they eventually come. I can feel my self-trust and my connection to inner guidance. My need is shifting away from always seeking external support, validation, or feedback to something much more intrinsic. I am feeling more and more self-contained and confident in who I am on my own. I am healing.

For the first few months of this new journey, I felt slow and heavy, and, most prevalently, sad. Without a man in my life though (or the pursuit of one), I have time to spend reading, feeling, and experimenting with new activities. I host a Wine, Women, and Wisteria event at my house, take a weekend trip with my daughter, work on house projects, and start planning a grand holiday season. At this halfway point, I find myself present much of the time. With each new awareness, I reach out to Gayle. She is like the perfect boyfriend, which is a funny thing to say since I've never had one of those. She is someone who is really interested in what is happening in my life, someone who is actually able to dialogue with me and cheer me on when I am making progress. She is the one I can rely on, and I am so grateful that she is holding my hand.

My journal is my other best friend. I find such solace in my early morning ritual of a cup of coffee and my journal. I write as soon as I wake up to stay connected to that sleepy place in my psyche that provides access to my deeper self. Early in the year, my writing was mostly about grief and loss, and then mostly about anger and resentment. Now, more graceful points of view, less harsh self-criticism, and more gentle kindness are showing up. I feel like layers of old clothes are dropping to the ground as I continue to walk away from a man and into myself. My whole being feels lighter as each layer falls to the floor. Whatever this new place is, I am enjoying it and want to spend my life safely in the confines of my cozy little home surrounded by my cozy friends.

David Whyte's poem "Everything Is Waiting for You" calls to me often during this time. I've seen him deliver this poem in person several times. Each time, the depth of his words and the clarity of his delivery allow this poem to seep into the deepest places of my being. In it, he compares aloneness to a heavy weight and tells the reader to set it down. I am doing just that.

We get our next letter from Dr. David.

Barb & Gayle:

How are you? I'm curious about your response to that question more than usual . . . mainly because one of my mentors, Sylvia Boorstein, author of the book It's Easier Than You Think: The Buddhist Way to Happiness, *said that when somebody asks her how she's doing, she replies, "I couldn't be better." Which is true; we are doing the best we can in any given moment. Your moods and happenings, for example, are fleeting. By realizing this, we/you can stay on the path without much distraction.*

Gayle, your freedom journey includes finding ways to let go. Letting go is hard, eh? But such independence on the other side! Do you think that you have become the sovereign in your own life? Can you more fully appreciate the inner peace you're experiencing, which counters the panic? The theme I was seeing, Gayle, was one of non-attachment, telling yourself that it is going to be okay. Gayle, there are skills in being able to "let go." The skills that you and Barb are expressing and acquiring will be valuable to others, particularly women. Are the letting go skills allowing more times when you are fully appreciating the present moment? Is it helping you to forgive yourself for past decisions, regrets? Is it allowing you to see the possibilities in every moment? Does it lead to more moments of joy?

Barb, you are on the same path and learning to let go. This is difficult at times because you have a great deal of contact with Mr. Mister and you love him. You don't want anybody else. Meditation helps along with reading and other forms of self-care, including spiritual practices and finding deeper meaning in life.

You are clearer and more confident (fear doesn't govern you as much as it did in the past). You said, "I get to choose. I'm on my path; anything is possible. I'm more capable and stronger than I thought possible." And you ARE fully committed to your path; no derailing here.

Yours along the path,
David

WINTER

All is well. Everything is working out for my highest good.
Out of this situation only good will come. I am safe.

—Louise Hay

We are halfway through our journey now. We've had highs, moments of true clarity, and feelings of being strong, independent whole women. At the same time, we've had many lows. The impending darkness of winter and the upcoming season of couple-ness—Christmas, New Year's, and Valentine's Day are right around the corner—so we make plans to travel to sunny places. But first, there is a major move ahead for Gayle.

20

—

The Move

Gayle

Normally, I wouldn't be grateful for a large moving van driving across my manicured front lawn and leaving behind twelve-inch-deep divots on both sides. Today, however, I am truly grateful. Why? Because now, the moving company's insurance will pay for the new sod that needs to be laid down, covering up the damage I did to the lawn just a few weeks earlier during a horrific snowstorm. I had tried to get my SUV up my sloped driveway, but when it became clear that I was stuck (all my tires would do is spin in the snow), I defaulted to calling my son, Cody, and even Greg to come help me. Sadly, neither of them was available.

I grabbed the snow shovel to dig myself out and found old boards to shove under the rear tires. It worked! I did it all by myself—no man involved. I felt so proud. The only problem was the muddy divots my spinning tires had created in the lawn right next to the "For Sale" sign.

My friend Mimi, the one who often invites me to her houseboat, is our real estate broker. She gets an all-cash, full-price offer on our home the first week it is up for sale. It all is happening so fast. For the most part, Greg has already been staying in a friend's guesthouse about fifteen minutes away.

Now I need to find my own place. On the night we accept the buyer's offer, Greg and I drive separately to our son's Friday night football game and sit apart. Normally, Barb would go with me to these Friday night games, but she is on another business trip.

I sit in the stands next to a couple who led our Bible study group (back when I had mistakenly thought being involved with couples who attended Bible study might help save my marriage). When I share the news that I need to find a rental, the wife tells me that a for-rent sign just went up that day on a super cute two-story, farmhouse-style home on a cul-de-sac in a sweet neighborhood across town. As she gives more details, I realize I might know the house she is referring to.

Three years earlier—before I jumped out of the airplane, before I began my emotional affair with Mr. Married, before grad school, before I realized my marriage was really over—I visited Mimi at an open house she was hosting. As I took in the surroundings, I remarked, "Wow, what great energy this house has. It's so homey. This would make a great divorce house." Mimi looked curiously at me, and I sort of wondered myself where that comment was coming from. At that time, needing a "divorce house" wasn't in my conscious awareness.

After the football game, I drive by that house. It's got a for-rent sign out front—it *is* the same place! I contact the property manager the next morning and, despite other potential tenants, I use my Gayle-force, backed by Greg's checkbook, to make sure I get the house. "When would be the best time to meet you to give you the deposit?" I ask the property manager, taking the position that the place is already mine. "I'm so excited to move in as soon as it works for the owner."

Mimi offers to vouch for me. She tells them that given my history as a responsible homeowner who also has the financial means (my husband's income) to cover the rent, I would be a perfect occupant.

Rental house secured? Check.

I hold it together just fine on moving day until my nice next-door neighbor Tom appears in the garage amid the moving mayhem.

"So, I guess you are really serious about this whole moving thing," Tom says. That's when it all hits me. I am leaving my custom-built dream home, where I had believed I would grow old with my husband, where my future grandchildren would visit and swim in the pool that we had yet to build. I hug Tom, a little longer than appropriate since I don't really know him that well, and instantly my throat tightens. Tears stream down my face and turn to sobs. I begin to cry, the kind of ugly crying where I can't catch my breath. I'm not able to stop, despite my embarrassment. I'm sure Tom has no idea what to do.

During all this, I recall that Mr. Married and I had originally planned that I would live alone for at least a year once I divorced and then we would begin to date each other. I am still pissed he is not even trying to contact me. *Is he even thinking of me?* I wonder. *Fucker!* I blame Mr. Married for not being here because he is "doing the right thing," but truthfully, I chose to spend a year without him.

Another shockwave of reality moves through me like one of those spinning scenes in the movies—the moving van and the thousands of little decisions in front of me.

One of the movers interrupts my sob fest. "What should I do with these old car parts, Mrs. Long?" he asks. "Did you want to pack this, or would you like me to?"

"I'll do it," I respond, thinking of the $222-an-hour packing charge.

Gratefully, my parents and Barb are here to help. Mom packs and cleans the refrigerator. Dad packs up the things in the laundry room. Barb holds me and cries with me throughout the day. I love her. Hollie brings sandwiches. Teri shows up later with champagne. My dad orders the salmon with butternut squash from Lefty's, the dish that has become a tradition for Barb and me to share, and opens a killer bottle of Windwalker Grand Chardonnay.

Barb eats with us at my family kitchen table in the new rental house. She is there for me. Our yellow lab Molly sleeps with Cody during his first night in our new home. DIRECTV and Comcast come in the morning. My Buddha is hung high on the wall. My favorite painting of Sand Harbor at Lake Tahoe has found a home. I feel safe, and I realize I am okay.

I love my new house.

21

You Should Have Let Him Love You

Barb

I am starting to be able to see myself traveling, living day to day, and having a life on my own. I also expect more challenges lay ahead. With the darkness of winter comes a deeper sense of connection with myself. I can feel myself going inward with the shortening of each day. I hear the message that I need to "heal the wound."

I am still spending a fair amount of time stuck on questions like, *Will Mr. Mister do what it takes? If not, who will be next? What will that be like? Who will I become?* And I still have the sense that I, alone, am never going to be enough. What if that thought could be stricken from the record? What if I am enough, have enough? What if I am complete? What freedom and happiness might come with a thought so radical?

I go to a hypnotherapist to see if I can get some clarity before entering the "Season of Couples." On the hypnotherapist's treatment table, I lay down and settle in. She speaks in a calm voice and starts a meditation-like process with me. She asks me to descend a ladder in my mind, farther, farther, and farther. At some point, I feel like I am deep inside myself. Strangely, I am aware of my body and my surroundings but also very relaxed. For example, I feel like I can raise my hand, but I'm so relaxed and peaceful that I don't want to. It is a delightful feeling, and I want to stay there for a long time.

Before the session, we spoke about what I was hoping to clear. I had explained a little bit about my history, the year without a man, and how I am looking for clarity, peace, and a sense of relief from the relentless pursuit of a man that I'd spent so much of my life on. While I am under, the hypnotherapist asks me to go back to the time when the issue began. I go back to my childhood, to when my father left.

"I'm there," I say. All of my years in therapy have taught me that my original wound was the moment he left. She asks me if this is the beginning.

"No," I reply, which surprises me.

"I want you to keep going back, further and further to the point of origin of this issue," she gently tells me. I feel myself moving through darkness and struggling to get through it, and then it's like I'm watching a movie scene right in front of me. I am no longer directing my thoughts but observing what I am being shown.

I see a beautiful young woman with brown hair, wearing a long brown dress like in an old Western movie. Her hat matches her outfit perfectly. She is put together but not fancy. I can tell she is strong but not bold, pretty but not made up, and she is arguing with a man right in the middle of a dirt street. She begins to hit him—not in a hurtful way, but in a frustrated way. She is trying to get a point across to him about something he isn't doing or being. She begins to hit him on his arms and chest. He uses his long arms to stop her. He wraps his arms around her to stop the hitting, and they are entangled for a minute. Finally, their arms separate, and they stand there looking at each other.

After I explain this to the hypnotherapist, she asks me to move forward in time and visit this woman when she is at the end of her life. Immediately, I am in a small room upstairs in an apartment in the same cowboy town that the young woman had been standing in when she was arguing with the young man. My point of view shifts, and I realize I am standing in the room next to the woman and she is looking up, directly at me. The woman is a bit heavier, still well-kept, with a long white braid along the right side of her head. She is wearing a white nightgown and is very weak. I can see that she is tired, but she is alert. The hypnotherapist then asks me what the woman wants to say to me. Just then, the woman reaches out, grabs my hand, and says directly to me, "You should have let him love you."

The old woman's words hit me like a ton of bricks. There is so much information in this one tiny sentence: "You should have let him love you." The therapist explains that I have just experienced a past life regression, which is when you see, hear, or feel memories of past lives you've lived.

On my way home, those words ring over and over in my head, *You should have let him love you.* Over the next few days, I begin to see all the times and all the ways I have made my partner the problem, the one who was wrong. The reality has been that my heart was not accessible and had never been open to being truly loved. But I couldn't see that then, so naturally I blamed my partners. All of them. If he only had a better job, if he was only a better communicator, if he was more interested in my perspective, blah dee blah dee motherfucking blah.

For the first time, I see that the problem is my inability to love or let love in. I have never allowed myself to be vulnerable.

I am the one who never let anyone in, into the real me. I have spent all my time and energy trying to figure out what has been right (or wrong) with them rather than looking at what was right (or wrong) with me. Fuck! Struck with truth again! Everything feels upside down. I am grateful for the new awareness but stung by the breadth and depth of my part in it.

22

The Holidays

Gayle

I have moved into my new home. My soon-to-be ex-husband and I are in the beginning stages of our divorce. I've begun my marriage and family therapist internship, seeing clients under supervision. I continue to see my own therapists, Joan and Dr. David. And I decide Christmas must be avoided at all costs.

Christmas in our house has traditionally been a big deal. Together, Greg and I used to hunt for the perfect tree that would nearly touch our cathedral ceiling. Outside, Greg would wrap trees in twinkly lights, and I would do my over-the-top decorating. This year, Sierra and Carley are coming home from college, Cody is in his last year of high school, and the house has been sold. There is no family home. The marriage is over. My new house is still filled with boxes, and Greg is in a small rental. I cannot begin to think about decorating or pretending. So we decide to take our family to Cabo San Lucas. Cabo is where we spent our honeymoon twenty-three years ago.

"Let's just go," I'd said to Greg. "We can get an all-inclusive package as our gift to the kids. We can get three rooms. One for you and Cody, one for the girls, and one for me." A wild idea, but amazingly, he agrees. Even though we never verbalized our thinking to each other, it seems obvious now that we were rationalizing the trip as a way to help ease the guilt we both shared over breaking up the family. Our kids are excited about the idea of spending the holidays on a sunny beach, so the trip to Mexico makes sense. Until we are actually there.

We all basically spend the entire week drunk. I am drunk. Greg is drunk. The kids are drunk.

On Christmas night, I walk down to the deserted pool alone, intoxicated. Quietly, I lay on one of the lounge chairs under a dark sky full of shining stars. In a moment of weakness, I text to Mr. Married: "I miss you." I push "Send," and out it goes into the universe as I think about how alone I am and how alone I feel. Almost immediately, a response comes back, as if from the dark, starry skies above me: "I miss you too." And there it is again—hope. A shared moment that I interpret as *he has not forgotten about me. He still loves me. There is still a chance.* I have initiated contact, and his response has sent me into a spin. I took a hit of my drug, and now I feel even worse.

The rest of the week is more of the same. Greg ignores me and spends the majority of the time in his room. The kids pretend they don't notice, and maybe they don't. We move mechanically from one day to the next until it is time to go home.

Back in California, I plan to spend New Year's Eve with Barb. We need a strategy because the last thing we want to be doing on New Year's Eve is sitting at home alone, even if we are together. We are proactively avoiding the possibility of a pity party. Just the idea of us in our bathrobes, eating potato chips and crying in our bottles of bubbly is enough to push us out the door.

We decide we will go to dinner and then see a show at the local performing arts center. Comedian Paula Poundstone is known for her openness and humor on topics ranging from life in San Francisco to parenting and politics. Seeing a female comedian with few boundaries sounds like the perfect way to ring in the New Year. This way, there will be no pressure to find a midnight kiss during "Auld Lang Syne."

Barb

On New Year's Eve, we sit down at a local Italian restaurant. Since our greatest pleasures these days are delicious food and cocktails (in moderation of course), I order the best eggplant parmesan I have ever had. Gayle has the fettuccine alfredo, made from a recipe passed down through generations by the owner's grandmother. We both order cosmopolitans, which are the perfect accompaniment to just about anything. Gayle takes a bite of pasta and literally moans. It's embarrassing. "Get a room!" I tell her. She laughs at her outward oralgasm and then fills me in on her botched attempt at family Christmas. I realize our holidays have been about as different as they could be.

Feeling empowered after Thanksgiving, I had claimed Christmas. Both of my children were home with me, and I made a traditional dinner with all their favorite dishes. Cooking is not my strong suit, but somehow, I created every dish associated with the holiday. I spent the entire day peeling potatoes, basting a bird, and making apple and pumpkin pie complete with decorated crusts with Sammy's help. I enjoyed every minute of it, and I did Christmas dinner all by myself. Everything came out perfectly. There was no drama, only love and joy. It was the best Christmas I can ever remember having.

I felt my power.

"Here's to us in the New Year," I say as Gayle and I finish dinner with a toast. As we try not to think about Mr. Mister or Mr. Married, we both laugh out loud. "Fuck those fuckers," we say in unison. We leave the restaurant and walk across the street to the comedy show. In our minds, we are the only women without dates on New Year's Eve. But as we walk into the theater, we realize that is absolutely not true. It makes us feel better to see so many single people out on New Year's Eve.

Paula Poundstone is exactly what we need. She tells funny stories about life with children and how difficult it is to grow up. "Growing up is not for babies," Paula says. How right she is. Gayle and I are still working on that.

We are both trying hard not to think about whom our fantasy men might be kissing tonight. It is the first year since we were teenagers that we are not kissing a man at midnight. Miraculously, we survive.

"See you in the morning!" Gayle says as the taxi picks her up. That's when I remember that Gayle and Hollie will be at my house the next morning for our annual New Year's Day event.

23

Dreaming Ahead

Barb

At precisely ten a.m., the doorbell rings, and Hollie is standing there with scissors, magazines, and glue. "I'm ready for a great year," she says.

"Me too!" I reply.

Gayle walks up with her hands full of magazines. "Me three," she adds with a giggle. We tell Hollie about our New Year's Eve with Paula Poundstone and then settle into our spots in my living room.

Years ago, I discovered the process of creating vision boards after completing a training with Mark Bryan, co-author of the book *The Artist's Way at Work*. Since then, leading vision board events has been part of my quest to tie my work and spiritual life closer together. This year feels more significant because the previous several months are proof of the power of setting intentions and developing the support necessary to move toward them.

We sit together in a circle with a warm fire blazing in the wood stove and relaxing spa music playing softly in the background. "Everyone, sit in a comfortable position, get centered, and breathe. Let's connect with our inner guidance and spiritual guides," I say quietly. We sit in silence for several minutes.

"When you are ready, open your eyes and begin."

Slowly each of us gets up and goes to the table now covered in magazines. The process is highly intuitive, so we work silently. Each of us goes through the publications, tearing out images and words that resonate with us without giving the process any conscious thought. I let the information come to me, allowing my subconscious mind and inner guide to speak. Then I set goals based on what comes to me (thanks to Dr. J's teaching). The room fills with the sounds of tearing paper. When each of us has a pile of torn images and words, we cut them neatly and begin arranging everything on individual pieces of poster board, again using only our intuition to guide us. Once complete, we each take a break for some tea or a snack, waiting for the others to finish.

"Who wants to go first?" I ask.

Over the next few minutes, each of us describes what we picked and how it was arranged. The words and images often reflect the person's journey very clearly to those of us watching and listening, but it is often hard for the person who made the board to see her journey until the rest of us give feedback and insights.

Last year, Gayle's entire board was covered with a variety of gorgeous men circling a giant diamond ring with a marriage proposal prominently displayed in the center and the words "Dreaming of His Affection" and "Up Against the Wall" (sexual innuendo intended). This year, the images reflect her accomplishments and a hope for discovery and adventure. It is much more about discovering herself and a happy and full life. An image of a dependable-looking, beautiful man is on the board, but he is off to one side rather than the center of attention. The words "Happy life," "Make fabulous you," and "No regrets" take prominence.

My board has girlfriends, getaway destinations, a message to live my best life, the bikini I hope to fit into again, and a handwritten message in the top left: "I choose freedom."

"Barb, you dream big," Gayle comments. "When you set your mind to something, it manifests."

I think of David Whyte's poem "Everything Is Waiting for You" and remember that I am not alone. I realize, here and now, in the presence of my girlfriends, that I began this journey feeling abandoned. Abandonment has been the story I have lived since my father left. That belief has kept me searching endlessly for a man to fix me, and that same belief has always kept me at a distance from most people. It reminds me of something Brené Brown wrote, "We grow up and learn to armor ourselves against feeling exposed, uncertain and vulnerable and then we hit adulthood and we realize to be the people that we want to be, we have to take all of this armor off, we have to put our weapons down and we have to show up and let ourselves be seen."

This morning, I feel like I have taken off my armor. I do feel intimacy. I feel my life. I feel who I really am all the way through my body. My daily practice of mindfulness and journaling has been a key to the locked door I didn't even know I was trapped behind. By taking the focus off finding that "one" key relationship, I find myself engaged with my friends at a deeper level. The friendships I am now creating include open, vulnerable conversations about spiritual topics, the meaning of relationships, and life itself. I want to hold on to this place of acceptance and openness and divine inspiration forever.

David Whyte's poem reminds me that everything is waiting for me.

From this place, I begin to see a better future: one that is focused on living from the inside out, from my own perspective, not the perspective of someone else. I can see all the ways, big and small, that I have looked to others to heal myself over and over, as if I was paying penance for some great sin. Relationship after relationship after relationship, I reached out desperately for someone, only to find the same dull pain I had always felt. Today, though, that wounded place inside me is healing.

We receive a letter from Dr. David in early January, acknowledging the changes that are taking place in us on this journey.

Dear Barb and Gayle,

Happy New Year! I hope the new year is continuing to bring forth some of the powerful developments that both of you have been making. I was struck by how much shift and movement there was in our last meeting.

Gayle, things were beginning to happen in a preferred direction: moving into the rental house, for example. There was a sense that you are letting go of fear and trusting that things will present themselves in ways that will be okay—that it is what it is. You feel lighter, more at peace, and are standing up straight. Are you in touch with your own strength of character as you are pursuing your life's mission?

Have you noticed and appreciated your journey? Do you see how you might inspire and empower others in believing in themselves? In what ways are you experiencing inner peace and freedom in your mind and body?

Barb, great job with, and kudos on, your continued transformation and spiritual awakening. Although it's been painful, particularly with your struggle with attachment to Mr. Mister, you are "in the flow." You are experiencing joy, insight, and love, often at a cellular level.

Remember fear's email to you and Gayle way back? I wonder what fear would say now.

Yours in this journey,
Dr. David

24

The Travel Cure

Barb

"We should plan a trip," I say to Gayle. "We could go somewhere sunny and warm. We could use my timeshare."

"That is a fabulous idea!" Gayle exclaims.

We consider a trip to Italy to play and experience decadent food. We could explore the Tuscan countryside while taking wine and cheese picnic breaks and writing about insights we have on our journey. We consider a trip to Sri Lanka, Dr. J's home country, where we would be able to delve into our spiritual life through meditation and yoga. Gratefully, we are blessed to feel like anything is possible. After fantasizing about re-creating Elizabeth Gilbert's journey in *Eat, Pray, Love*, practicality and convenience win out, and we decide a week in Acapulco will do.

With the exception of my solo trip to Hawaii earlier in the year, I've done all of my vacation travel with a partner. It even sounds funny to me as I write it now. I love to travel and have been fortunate enough to have done quite a bit of it because of my career. Surviving this year without a man would be a challenge if I didn't have someone to travel with for fun. Lucky for me, Gayle loves to travel as well, and she proves to be a more effective travel partner than the men I've had so far in my life. She is great at details and mapping out the plan, which I appreciate.

Although I always had the desire for my husband to be my perfect traveling partner, I always did the planning. I would have the idea to go on vacation, figure out where to go, and then manage the details. This time, Gayle does a lot of the planning, and that is sweet relief for me. Gayle has never been on a major trip without her husband, nor has she ever been on a trip to a romantic destination without a man. I remind her that we're in it together.

I'm a Hilton/United/Avis girl, having traveled so frequently with them for work. Preferred travel status may seem like a silly thing to covet, but when you have it, traveling becomes a lot easier. I know where the airline check-in counters are in the airports that I frequent. I know what the hotel room and amenities will be like when I check-in, and I know how to get to the rental car in the fastest way possible. I use the same companies over and over, so I know them and they know me. They reward me with free travel, free stays, and free upgrades.

Several years back, I bought a timeshare at Hilton because it was an easy extension of my long-standing Hilton hotel relationship. I know what to expect when I book my condo, just like when I book my hotels. Generally speaking, all is good. Except, apparently, in Acapulco.

Gayle and I arrive ready for a week of sand and sun. The condo is a partner hotel to Hilton and sits right at the end of a peninsula with beautiful deep blue water surrounding it. The lobby is open to the outside, so we can smell the sea air. The air is warm, and the sun is high. As we make our way up a few floors, I am looking forward to the type of unit I have come to expect: two bedrooms with separate baths, an open kitchen, and a cozy living room looking out over the water. I am excited to look out the big windows and let all that gorgeous sunshine pour over me. We open the door and walk in.

This place is dark, small, and gloomy. It smells old and musty. The bathtub is dingy and has broken tile. The kitchen is dirty. We hear screaming children coming from the kiddy pool right outside the window. My first thought is that our whole vacation is ruined. I can't live in this place for a whole week. My next thought is *Shit, now what?* My first reaction to a challenging situation is usually to panic. Fortunately, I've learned this about myself, so I am able to take a breath and turn to Gayle.

The look on Gayle's face is a cross between a frown and a smile—let's call it a frile. Her lips are trying to smile, but the frown is pulling them down so there is a straight line where her mouth is supposed to be. Her eyebrows are arched like she is trying to make her whole face smile—it isn't working. I'm sure she is also thinking, *This is a shithole, and I don't want to stay here.*

"This is not going to work," I say.

Gayle's frile turns into a look of concern. "What do you think we can do?" she asks.

"We can let them know they've made a mistake," I answer. So, we take our bags and go back down to the registration desk.

"We need a different unit," I state plainly to the sweet young lady at the front desk. She frowns and lets us know there is nothing she can do. We ask to speak to the manager.

"Is there a problem?" Mario the manager asks.

Hell, yes, there is a problem. Your rooms are disgusting, is what plays out in my head, but out loud I simply explain, "These are not the accommodations I have come to expect as an owner of Hilton. Surely, there must be a mistake."

"You booked this through your timeshare, and while we are a partner, their deal is their deal. You have a two-bedroom unit for a week, and that is what we have given you."

We thank him for his time and walk away more than a bit discouraged. It seems as though we have hit a dead-end, so we do what any other capable, powerful person would do, we go to the pool bar. With a margarita in my hand and some killer guacamole in front of me, I decide to call Hilton. It is late in Florida (where they are based), but I get someone on the phone.

"Hello," I begin. "We are at the Fiesta Americana in Acapulco, and it is not up to Hilton standards—it's really not. Is there anything you can do for us? Can you put us in a Hilton hotel?"

"We don't have any Hilton properties in Acapulco."

"Where is the closest Hilton?"

"Cabo San Lucas."

I look over at Gayle. "We can fly there tomorrow," I say, and she nods in agreement. Okay, things are looking up, we can escape Acapulco and get to Cabo. We understand it will cost some money for the flight, but this vacation is part of our strategy for staying on track with all that we are going through this year. We are not willing to give up the idea.

We go back to the front desk to tell Mario we will be leaving, but he interrupts. "I think we have a possible solution. Come with me." We follow him to the elevator. We go up, up, and up some more, all the way to the top floor. *Maybe this'll be nicer*, I think. Out of the elevator and down the hall we walk and walk and walk. Now, one thing I've learned after staying in a bunch of hotels is that the farther you walk down the hall, the better. End-of-the-hall rooms often give you better views and sometimes corner windows. At the very end of the hall, he opens the door. "Will this work for you ladies?" he asks.

We stand there looking down a long, marble-tiled floor toward a magnificent living room and nearly explode with excitement inside while staying super cool on the outside. We walk down the hall, touring bedroom one and bedroom two, noting each has a tiled walk-in shower as well as its own private balcony. The marble tile runs throughout and into the stunning granite kitchen. The dining table has settings for six. As Mario turns his back to us to open the sliding glass door to the veranda, which crosses half the length of the building, Gayle and I make eye contact and simultaneously mouth the words, *Oh my God*. It feels as if we are leaning out over the blue of the ocean itself.

"The master suite is this way," he says and leads us down another hall. We wonder if he thinks we are a couple. It's becoming a thing—people mistaking us for a couple rather than just two single women who aren't currently interested in finding or being in a romantic relationship. Mario shows us to the spectacular room about half the size of my entire house.

"Will this work for you?" he asks. I give him a casual smile and nod. "How much more would you be willing to spend?" I look over at Gayle who is fiercely trying to contain herself.

"The thing is, Mario, we are both going through divorces right now and really just need to escape from our hometowns to try to relax and forget about everything. We don't really have a lot of extra money. Do you think $200 would be enough?"

Mario smiles and shakes his head. Gayle's frile begins to reappear when he pauses and then says with a smile, "No additional charges. This is our gift to you."

"Thank you so much," we both say calmly, and he leaves us standing in the living area. Once we are sure he is far enough away, we begin screaming with delight. "Oh my God! What just happened?" I ask.

"We just manifested a penthouse suite with marble floors and epic views of Acapulco," Gayle replies. "This vacation is going to be fantastic!"

The best part is we have done this on our own. No man has come to the rescue, and no man has been necessary. (Mario the hotel manager doesn't count, we tell ourselves.)

Gayle

Barb has got this traveling thing down to a science. I stick close by her side and feel comfortable and secure knowing she is in charge.

Being a night owl, I am awake and alone in my room for hours after Barb goes to bed. It is from the comfort of my private king-sized bed that I find the need to write Mr. Married a letter that I will never send. Witnessing couples frolicking and kissing in the warm ocean water earlier in the day brings those old longings right back to the surface. "Someday" becomes my mantra. I live for the future. This is when my obsessive thoughts resurface, and my laptop becomes my most intimate companion. These letters tend to start with me writing my feelings and thoughts to Mr. Married, but these days, my writing usually ends with helpful guidance from my higher self.

> *Dear Mr. Married,*
>
> *I miss you so much. I have fantasies of your arms around me and of you holding me and telling me that everything will be okay. If only that were reality. Life is hard right in the space between falling off a cliff and landing safely on the ground. Against all odds, I still hold loving thoughts of you in my heart. I've learned so many lessons this past year. I've grown so much, and I've become someone who is all about treating myself with loving-kindness. I have faith that all will be well. What is meant to be WILL be. I am closing my eyes and imagining your lips kissing mine. . . .*

Somehow, I am still not ready to let go of the dream on one level, while on another level, I fully realize he's just not that into me. My higher self tells me: *Please get over him and move on for your own good. Stop looking back. It doesn't serve you. You deserve a man who loves and adores you and makes sacrifices to be with you. A man who gets how amazing you are, connects with you, and will make your future so much richer. Release completely. Let the idea of him go forever. You have grieved long enough. Seriously. Listen to your guides. You are so much farther down the path than you realize.*

I fall asleep, struggling but grateful to be hearing my higher self so much more clearly than the longings I still hold on to. My grip is loosening, but my fingers are still closed.

Barb

We spend the next several days taking in the sights and loung-ing for hours by the pool. I am reading Pema Chödrön's *When Things Fall Apart*, and Gayle is reading *If the Buddha Dated*, which I had finished earlier in the year. We both enjoy learn-ing and are open to many points of view. Often, when we find an interesting idea, we read it aloud to one another, which usually evolves into a long and stimulating conversation.

One day lying poolside by the beautiful blue water, I look up from Chödrön's book and say to Gayle, "Listen to this: 'The experience of certain feelings can seem particularly preg-nant with desire for resolution: loneliness, boredom, anxiety. Unless we can relax with these feelings, it is very hard to stay in the middle when we experience them. We want victory or defeat, praise or blame. If someone abandons us, we don't want to be with that raw discomfort. Instead, we conjure up a familiar identity of ourselves as hapless victim or maybe we avoid the rawness by acting out and righteously telling the person how messed up he or she is. We automatically want to cover over the pain in one way or another.'

"This is what we are going through right now. She then follows with the Katagiri Roshi quote, 'One can be lonely and not tossed away by it.'"

"Oh my God, that is so good," Gayle responds.

We finish our cocktails, diving deep into Pema's concept of loneliness and resting in the middle. We are experiencing a river of insights about ourselves, our love lives, and all our relationships. We sit in silence looking out over the vast, blue sea. The rhythm of the ocean can be so healing: When you are happy, it moves; when you are frustrated, it moves; and when you are angry, it moves. The consistent rhythm of the ocean is a salve for me. It is patient, kind, and everlasting.

One of the quotes I appreciate most during this time is something I heard from Jane Fonda. She said, "We are not meant to be perfect; we are meant to be whole." This is my direction, my goal—to be complete. Jane Fonda also said that when she went through a divorce, she had to "walk close to the wall" and move slowly, because finding balance on a new path is often tentative. I appreciate her words now as I feel the same need to walk close to the wall and take great care of myself. My morning meditation practice helps me keep my promise that I will go slowly so I can find and maintain a new equilibrium.

Through so much of my life, my equilibrium has been off. When we experience big losses early in our lives and don't have the support systems in place to heal those emotional wounds, we create coping mechanisms to survive. My earliest coping mechanisms were independence, drive, and strength. I am fortunate that my choices were ones that our culture rewards me for having rather than something more destructive like alcoholism or drug addiction, which could have easily been my path with alcoholism in my family history. My drive led me to create a workaholic lifestyle, which has given me the financial independence I need to feel safe.

My addiction to romantic relationships has been my second coping mechanism. It allowed me to always have someone there so I wouldn't feel lonely even though I never really feel connected relationally. Until Mr. Mister, of course. With him, I'd experienced emotional and spiritual connection. And yet he was unavailable to be with me. Here on vacation, I am living without the protection of those two strategies. I am becoming a steady stream of energy, ebbing and flowing naturally, just like the waves I am staring at.

As we are enjoying the perfection of the moment, Gayle pops up from her chaise lounge and says, "We should find some kind of symbol to memorialize this journey, Barb. Like a ring or something like that."

"People already seem to think we are a couple." I laugh. "We may as well get the ring."

"Not a wedding ring," Gayle protests. "More like something big and contemporary and silver, with maybe a stone or two of some kind. After all, who ever said only married women can sport a ring on their left ring finger? Let's celebrate being single and the fact we have no interest in dating!"

The hotel offers free umbrellas, and, with clouds gathering in the sky, we grab one as we head out on a long walk through the uneven streets lined with local shops, bars, and cafés. The holidays are over, and there aren't many tourists about. This puts more pressure on us to respond to the incessant shouts of the locals attempting to lure us into their nearly empty establishments.

"Come in, pretty ladies, and eat at my restaurant," they call.

"Come drink here!"

"Cocktails for you?"

Over those few days in Mexico, we eat good food and meet interesting people without having to constantly wonder, *Is he the one? Is he the one?* We are entirely ourselves as we walk through the open-air shopping markets, looking for treasures to bring home. We wander far away from the hotel, through the winding streets of Acapulco, shopping our way through outdoor market after outdoor market. But we cannot find the right ring.

We have been walking for quite some time in our flip-flops and shorts when it begins to rain. And then it begins to rain *hard*. We huddle together, clutching our small umbrella, which offers little shelter from the torrential downpour.

What we experience next seems like a scene from a natural disaster movie or the back lot at Universal Studios. Water surges toward us. With inadequate drainage, the water coming between the buildings, off the roofs, and even from underneath the underdeveloped streets quickly becomes a dirty, running torrent. We stand in the middle of it all, afraid to head back the way we came, and afraid to move forward.

"I'm going to lose my flip-flops!" Gayle yells as the filthy water flowing down the sloped street tries to steal them from her feet. Then, before we can understand how or why, we begin to laugh. We are soaked to the bone, and all I can think about is the fact that we are probably treading through raw sewage. "God, I hope this isn't sewer water! Oh God, I hope this isn't sewer water!" I begin to panic-repeat.

Gayle announces, "Well, I am sure it is sewage water. This is the hydro-apocalypse." That makes us laugh even more.

"Barb!" Gayle exclaims between gasps of laughter, "The idea that you, Miss Barb DeHart, who wears stylish, cleaned, and pressed clothes at all times, is traipsing through dirty sewage water in a rainstorm is more than I can bear."

Gayle can't finish her next sentence as she begins laughing uncontrollably and bends over, letting go of the umbrella. "Oh my God," she continues snorting with laughter, "I'm peeing!"

Now I am chanting, "Oh God, I hope this isn't sewer water!" and Gayle is repeating, "I'm peeing; I can't stop peeing!" So of course, we are walking in it. We are walking in Gayle's pee and quite possibly the pee of all of Acapulco.

I have never laughed so hard in my life. This is not at all the classy Gayle-and-Barb-go-on-vacation scene we had planned. It is, however, the funniest moment of the year and one we still laugh out loud about when we recall it. This is the joy of our deepened friendship—completely ourselves, completely authentic, bonding over something completely ridiculous.

The sun comes out minutes later and, in a move that is very out of character for us, we continue on our quest for jewelry rather than returning to our condo to clean up. We figure, "When in Acapulco . . ."

25

Valentine's Day

Gayle

Only a few weeks after Acapulco, it's time to repack our bags. Our next adventure to break up the loneliness of winter is for Hollie's fiftieth birthday, which is on Valentine's Day. We will escape Valentine's Day at home by running to Miami for a few days before boarding a cruise ship with a group of Hollie's friends. With celebration in mind, we order champagne on the plane and never look back. As soon as we land, we can almost smell the money in South Beach. It's full of beautiful people and has an over-the-top hedonism that we settle right into.

We let our intuition guide us through South Beach. We find a hotel that is the perfect combination of style, location, and price, and as a bonus, comes with a rooftop pool. We walk the boardwalk and take in the beach and shops and restaurants. It is wonderful to be aware of men who are checking us out because, for this moment, it is a game we are not playing. We have no interest, no need to posture, no need to wonder if they will approach. It is flattering to have the attention but freeing to know nothing will come of it.

When a young, wealthy man asks Barb to spend the day with him at an exclusive resort spa, she has no trouble saying, "No, thank you." No wondering, no what-ifs. We settle into the sunny beach and pool by day, enjoying fabulous food and swanky clubs at night.

Barb

Although we are new to the club scene, with Gayle's sense of entitlement firmly in hand, we stride confidently past the red velvet stanchions and the handsome bouncer into flashing colorful lights and loud music. Gayle sees a section of empty seats.

"Look, they saved room just for us," she says with a smile. We sit down. Just then, a server approaches and condescendingly explains that we are in a private area that can be reserved for five hundred dollars. "It does come with a personal attendant and a bottle of Stoli," she adds.

Not letting this burst our bubble, we reluctantly move to the bar with the rest of the ordinary patrons. A few cosmos later, we are up and dancing without a care in the world.

The next day, as we are wandering the streets of this beautiful city, we find ourselves on the famous Millionaire's Row, luxurious condos on one side and a harbor full of yachts on the other. When I see that this is the week of the Miami International Yacht Show, I say playfully, "Let's go yacht shopping."

We wander down to the harbor and onto the first of several yachts. We freely walk onto a fifty-footer and then onto a seventy-two-footer made by Grand Banks. We are like little girls playing dress up, pretending that these are ours. We move the velvet ropes out of our way, disregard the "do not sit here" signs, and—careful not to cause any damage—take pictures of ourselves and each other. We are clearly outside our weight class in the Lifestyle of the Rich and Famous, but we have fun acting as-if. Our fantasy is cut a bit short when an agent stops us on the dock of a gorgeous 150-foot five-million-dollar yacht.

At this point, the gig is up. Sitting at a desk set up on the dock, the agent says to us, "You ladies need to bring your broker and prequalify before being given permission to come aboard." Though we do our best to dress the part, Banana Republic couture is not the level of attire these people are looking for.

"Well," I say, "when I am ready to purchase, don't you want us to call on you?"

"Nice try," is the response. They are having none of it. "You know," Gayle wonders as we walk away, "Do you think they would be questioning our credibility if we had men with us?" It doesn't really matter. Just like the VIP section of the nightclub, this is not our place, and these are not our people.

We head to an outdoor café for dinner and happen upon an adorable man dressed in a bright pink silk shirt and crisp white summer slacks, sitting alone and holding an "I Love You" heart-shaped balloon.

"Happy Valentine's Day," we say in unison.

We are so relieved to be away from home and away from the pressure of having to find the right card for our estranged partners or having to bear the weight of expectations for a romantic evening. Thoughts of Mr. Mister or Mr. Married are far from our minds tonight. We happily sit down next to the man and strike up a conversation. Assuming we are a couple, he responds, "Happy Love Day."

"Are you alone?" Gayle asks.

"Yes, and missing my boyfriend terribly," he replies. "He's away on business. Are you two celebrating?"

We look at each other, and I respond, "Well, yes, but we aren't a couple. We are actually getting ready to go on a cruise to celebrate our girlfriend's birthday. We are celebrating love, just not romantic love."

We invite him to join us. We tell him about our year without a man and how great it feels to be away from our small town, where we would have inevitably run into people we know who are in love or pretending to be in love. "Fuck Valentine's Day," we tell him. He laughs and becomes the loveliest part of our evening. If we'd been lamenting our singleness or focused on finding a flirtatious encounter, we'd have never met this unexpected, delightful dinner companion.

Gayle

The next day we meet up with Hollie and her friends, thirteen of us who are connected to her in some way. Having never been on a cruise, as we walk up the ramp to the ship, we feel like cattle being herded. "Mooooo . . ," I groan as I look at Barb. Our concern is building as we walk down a long, dark hallway and look into the rooms to our left, which are small and dark and have only one small porthole for a window—until we open the door to the suite Barb and I will be sharing. We step out onto our balcony and realize Hollie has booked seven rooms almost in a row, excepting one unknown couple in the middle of the group. This isn't a problem—until we learn more about them.

We spend our first night at sea drinking, dancing, and sharing stories as we get to know the people in Hollie's party.

Happily, we are not the only pair of women in the group. In the wee hours, we wake up to the sound of deep moans coming through the thin wall from the mystery couple next door. The sound of sex lasts longer than what we remember as being normal. Nearly eight months into the year without a man—and without sex—the noise from next door pounds the reminder into my brain. We both lay quietly, hoping the moment will end.

"Are you awake?" I whisper.

"Yes, who could sleep through that?" Barb replies.

"Oh, thank God you can hear it too. I was afraid it was just me."

"It feels a little awkward to just lay here listening."

"I just wish they would shut the fuck up! Enough already." "Show-offs."

We both lay there, trying to block out the sound of what is obviously multiple orgasms, for an impressive length of time. "God, I want that," I say. "It has been so long." Eventually, the sex noises end, and we drift back to sleep.

The next morning, we meet our noisy neighbors and discover they have only been dating for a month. *Of course,* I think, catching Barb's eye. *New romance, new sex.* We hate them just a little.

As it happens, that would not be the last time we would be privy to the primal sounds of their lovemaking. It starts to annoy us. We are more than over it when a couple of days later, after a long afternoon in the sun, we return to our cabin for a nap, only to hear the sounds of sex beginning again.

"That's it!" Barb says. "I am going to make every sound she makes."

"Mmmmm oh," says the woman next door.

"Mmmmm oh," Barb replies.

I join in, and we create a chorus.

"Oh God," screams our neighbor.

"OH GOD," screams Barb.

"Oh God," we scream together.

"AHHHH!"

"AHHHH!"

"AHHHH!"

On it goes, minute after minute, for a full hour. Lost in their stupid fucking bliss, however, our neighbors never even hear us and carry on uninhibited. Finally, they stop, and so do we. Feeling exhausted and relieved that it's over, we drift into a pleasant afternoon slumber.

Barb

We spend the next day on a private beach at a club in Cozumel, drinking tiny Coronas that we order by the bucket. We eat nachos and hang out on one of the large wooden, canopied beach beds on the sand. The party scene in front of us is made up of mostly drunk, hot twenty-somethings, lathered in suntan oil, dancing to the live Jimmy Buffett–style band. One young guy picks me out of the crowd and starts flirting. I could probably be his mother. But I play along without a single self-conscious, curious, or sex-driven thought. The attention is flattering, but I'm not going down that road (though I would have in the past).

After Gayle and I nap on the beach bed, we hurry back to the ship for the captain's dinner. We are suntanned and still a little tipsy. We love getting dressed up, so we are excited to show off some new purchases we made in South Beach. I can't wait to wear my black satin Kenneth Cole pencil skirt with my white silk, tailored jacket. Gayle puts on a little black dress made of sequins. She adorns herself with several giant cocktail rings and big, sparkling chandelier earrings. Grabbing her rainbow sequined purse as we head out the door, she stops, looks down at her bare wrists, and says, "I think I need more bling."

I look up, and in a deadpan reply, "Gayle, you are wearing a sequined dress. I think you have bling covered." We both burst into laughter and walk out of the room. Seated with our new friends at our last cruise dinner, we are feeling confident and happy. We've made it past Valentine's Day—and we actually had fun doing it.

We leave the sun of Florida and return home to a snowstorm unlike any we have seen in years. Several feet of fresh snow cover the ground. The independence and self-reliance that we experienced on our vacations is one thing. But now we are back to the harsh reality of cold winter days and nights, which we will need to experience and handle on our own.

26

Day 272

Gayle

Once I saw a guy on match.com who said in his profile: "Don't bother contacting me if you are still hung up on your old husband/boyfriend/lover." Nine months into the journey, and I am still struggling to let go of the fantasy of Mr. Married. It makes me sick to my stomach to realize the truth: that I am still just up there circling the landing strip. I haven't allowed myself to truly fly high and experience freedom.

I am 272 days into this year without a man, and I haven't fucking left the airport yet! I am in a holding pattern, hanging on to the possibility that Mr. Married will choose me. Every day, I still allow my heart to ache over the reality that he hasn't. I seem to hurt more as the days go by, even as the illusion becomes more apparent and the odds of us being together grow slimmer. *What a fucker he is,* I think. Yet here I am crying, still stuck hoping that when this year without a man is over, he will make himself available to me. It's pathetic! I am smart and beautiful, and I have so much love to give to another person. *Where are you?* I think constantly. *Who are you? I know you are there, somewhere. Will you ever show up in my life?*

The guy on match.com is right. I have to get out of this

holding pattern and fly away. This circling is not attractive, and it's not fun.

How do I let go of my attachment to this idea that Mr. Married is the one? How do I truly and completely give myself permission to accept with 100 percent certainty that he is never going to be the one? If I don't allow myself to fly away and experience the freedom of being fully in relationship with myself, I will never discover the man I am meant to be with.

I can hear the voice in my head yelling at me, *You want a man who wants to shout to the world how much he loves you! HE IS NOT THAT MAN. WAKE UP! You are the captain. You are the pilot. Assume control of your destiny. You have been secured for takeoff. Release the final lock on your wheels. He is never going to do it for you. Only you can give the command for takeoff. You are ready, okay? Get set. . . . Now, GO!*

On a cold and rainy day in March, I run into Mr. Married outside of the local market. Just seeing him takes my breath away. And then he breaks my heart for the last time.

"Hi," I stammer. We begin an awkward conversation. "How's it going?"

"Fine," he answers automatically. And just as I did that Halloween evening with Barb, I stop him, take his hand, look in his eyes, and say, "No. Really. How are you?"

My words have the same effect now as they did back then. He stops the superficial chatter and tells me the truth. "Honestly, I am the best I have been in a very long time. I owe it to you, Gayle. You helped me to realize real relationships can exist. You taught me how to love. I am committed to making my marriage work. I do not intend to leave my marriage. . . ."

I don't hear anything he says after that. The irony is not lost on me that the choice he has made is the very choice I wished Greg had made about us. Mr. Married is becoming a man of integrity, a man of commitment, just not with me.

Somehow, I manage to smile and say back, "I'm really happy for you." What I'm really feeling is utter disbelief. *How can you not choose me?! You were supposed to be there for me at the end of this year!* I turn and walk away, surprised my shaking legs carry me. *What a motherfucking fucker.* I leave the grocery store parking lot, numb from the cold air and the frigid reality of my conversation with Mr. Married.

I go home and book a trip to stay with childhood friends in Laguna Beach so I can clear my head and thaw out. Alone on the beach a few days later, I finally allow myself to grieve. I pull my journal out of my beach bag and write, allowing some soft tears to release behind my dark sunglasses.

One should never underestimate the cunning power of denial. Denial is very smart and knows how to trick your brain in its efforts to hold off your inevitable pain. Once the shield of denial is removed, the truth is all that is left. Truth, standing there naked, drops the wet towel of denial into a heap on the floor. It took Mr. Married's direct words to me that he does not intend to leave his wife to shake me awake. It took hearing Greg have sex with another woman to get—without a shadow of a doubt—that my marriage was over. Denial has been trying to protect me from a broken heart, from pain. The problem with denial is that it is a block, an impediment to moving forward.

Now, at this moment, here on this beach, I am no longer in denial of the truth. There is no "us." There are no more dreams to cling to.

This is a private grief, a private mourning. This is not the kind of loss where people are going to drop by with casseroles or send sympathy cards. If there are flowers on the counter, it is because I bought them for myself. That is the reality of facing the loss of a secret relationship.

Mr. Married had the audacity to send me a "poke" on Facebook yesterday. I could feel my anger bubble up and stopped myself from replying with a "Fuck You." How dare he "poke" me; it's the least intimate thing he could do. Talk about crumbs. If telling me in person that he was staying with his wife didn't put the final nail in the coffin of possibilities, this sure did. *Fucker! I deserve so much better!*

On my lonely beach chair, I find myself wondering, *Why hide from the truth? Why is that so scary?* Then it comes to me, clear as day: Fear is why. My fear of being alone. In this moment, that fear finally strikes me as odd. While I have been so busy being afraid to be alone, at the same time, I have been . . . ALONE. So do I really have anything to be afraid of at all?

"And the truth shall set you free" indeed! I should thank Mr. Married for finally telling me the truth. Happiness is not going to be found "out there," in a man or a job or money or my kids. Happiness is not there on the outside; it is on the inside. With this new awareness, I can stop my desperate search and rescue mission for security and comfort. Now it is time to go into the pain, to really grieve, to let go, and once again, to let God guide me. I am not alone. I have divine support. Fear of being alone is an illusion because "being alone" is an illusion; therefore, fear in this case does not exist. Fear is truly, after all, as they say in twelve-step programs, false evidence appearing real.

I stay on the beach until the sun sets. It is beautiful. Walking back to my car, I pass a store window and notice my reflection. I can see how much I have changed. I am thin, fit, and alone. In dropping the relationships that haven't served me and my attachment to them, I have dropped physical weight as well. I no longer need to hold those extra pounds for protection. I realize I am enough.

I am reminded of a David Whyte quote:

One of the difficulties of leaving a relationship is not so much, at the end, leaving the person themselves—because, by that time, you're ready to go; what's difficult is leaving the dreams that you shared together. And you know that somehow—no matter who you meet in your life in the future, and no matter what species of happiness you would share with them—you will never, ever share those particular dreams again, with that particular tonality and coloration. And so, there is a lovely and powerful form of grief there that is the ultimate giving away in order to simultaneously make space for another form of re-imagination.

Once back home, we receive another timely Dr. David letter.

Barb and Gayle,
How are both of you? Time is going by fast! Here are some thoughts as

winter comes to an end and we get closer to meeting again.

Gayle, in our meeting in January, you shared your ongoing journey of courage and growth. Fear is unremitting and merciless in its efforts to deter you. It asks you:

Can you live alone and support yourself?

What if you are alone for good?

Will you find a man?

Yet, with each one of these questions, your response is clear and defiant. You are in touch with courage. You fear there is no real ground to stand on, but you are moving forward anyway. The habits that fear recruited you into are withering away; you are freeing yourself from its grip. No longer are you defining yourself as just a mother and wife. There's a new identity emerging.

Since our most recent meeting, what efforts have fear made to make a comeback? What does it try to whisper in your ear? What efforts are you making to stay on course? What are you appreciating about you?

A friend of mine recently bought me a refrigerator magnet with the saying:

If I am not happy

in this time and place,

then I am not paying attention.

The saying makes me think of you, Barb. You are living out that saying. Barb, you are also in a space of giving back to others and selflessness. Your journey of courage, of letting go and gaining new insights, is having a ripple effect on others around you, including Gayle.

These new insights are helping you realize that your relationship with Mr. Mister was "delicious in all its dysfunction." It is so intoxicating to stay in that kind of relationship; yet, not letting desire filter and distort, you realize that Mr. Mister is asleep. You want a man who is awake.

Gayle and Barb, your collective and individual path is an un-stoppable force now. And it is based on a healthy interdependence, rather than an unhealthy dependence. June is looming closer. Can you believe it!?

See you two soon.

Yours in solidarity,
Dr. David

Barb

I write back to Dr. David, telling him that tonight was the perfect night to receive this. I've spent much of the last couple of weeks in an intense funk because recent interactions with Mr. Mister at work have thrown off my equilibrium. I have found it increasingly difficult to continue my daily interactions with those who are asleep—people who give me conditioned responses, people who show no depth or authenticity. The pretense of those kinds of conversations is taking its toll on me, and I find myself exhausted by it.

I know that this is all for my own good—that I'm moving to a deeper place where I'm comfortable with vulnerability. I am beginning to take more graceful points of view about myself and others. I am functioning less from self-criticism and more from loving-kindness. It is important to record these times of strength and clarity. In the down times, I forget that those ever existed.

My inner voice is small and weak, but it is there and getting stronger. My new skin is yet to be revealed, but I am clear that I am becoming more authentic. This path is my destiny. I am willing to go where it takes me. I am letting go of every outcome I had planned. I am here. I am present. *Now* is a lovely place to be.

My spiritual, intellectual, and emotional journey has led me to the top of a mountain where I now feel at home. It has been my practice until now to leave my mountain to meet the men in my life. I would walk down (okay, run) to meet them and quickly forget that my mountain ever existed. I would deny my truths, my desires, the core of my being, to be with a man who wanted me. I would forget my visions, my journey, and my own life. And then I would go to work turning my current man into someone who wanted to be on my mountain with me. I would work hard to turn him into something that he wasn't. I will not do that again.

The beauty of today is that I can see this clearly, and I choose to stay up top. I won't walk down the mountain for anyone. I trust that if there is a man who wants to join me up here where the air is clean, the sun is warm, and the views are epic, that he will. And I will be here to welcome him.

SPRING

*If you change the way you look at things, the things you
look at change.*

—Wayne Dyer

We are in the home stretch now. The questions we are asking
now are so much deeper and more profound than the ones we
started with. We have dug in the soil of our hearts to pull out
the weeds that strangled our relationships with ourselves. We
have planted new seeds, and the sprouts are showing. They are
tender and young; we still have to treat them with care. We
have made it this far. What's a few more months to reach the
finish line?

27

The Final Season

Gayle

Back in town after my grieving trip to Laguna Beach, everything about me feels lighter. It is a sunny spring day, and I am driving through town on my way to Barb's deck to study for my final exams to become a fully licensed marriage and family therapist. The windows are down, and I'm singing along to Uncle Kracker's "Smile" on the radio. I am thinking about a conversation I had in therapy with Joan about loneliness and being alone. Joan says that we are really "all-one," and that feeling of aloneness comes when we feel separate from ourselves. In this moment, I smile and realize that I really am happy and content with myself.

In the past, those feelings only came from my connection with someone else, never from an internal connection to myself. Right now I feel like I am in love—in love with myself! I am alone, yet I feel all-one. No man is in the empty seat beside me, yet I feel pure joy. This must be what all the self-help experts mean when they say that we have to learn to love ourselves before we can truly love another. I feel totally connected to my pure Self. Now I get it.

Fewer than ninety days to go. While Barb and I are reflecting on how far we have come, we are also looking at how much we have to look forward to. We used to see a relationship as the main course, but now we realize it should be just one small part of our lives, a side dish. For Barb, the reality of allowing herself to be vulnerable is still a stretch. There is no question she has grown. She has learned so much about the "why" of her need and the "how" of being on her own, but she has yet to try allowing vulnerability into a relationship.

For me, I have nothing left to hold on to now but myself. I am alone and realize I have come a long way from the completely codependent woman who began this journey. Now living on my own, paying my own bills, and interning as a therapist, I am supporting myself and living single.

I just wish I didn't have to.

So I am looking forward to dating. I fully expect a pile of applicants waiting for me on June first. I am ready to move on. As soon as I realize that expectation, the truth hits me: waiting to be chosen is what I always wanted from my father, and then from my husband, and then from Mr. Married. No one is making me a priority. I am the only one capable of doing that. I have to be my own advocate. I am the one to make myself the first priority. I realize I need to be the most important person in my life.

Barb

I can't believe we are in the final season. I am not sure I want it to end. There is so much freedom in focusing only on myself and my children and my friends. I have proven I am capable of being on my own. I don't need a man to complete me. I really am the perfect whole and complete person I was searching for. It is important that I hold on to me when the next relationship comes along.

In the spirit of independence, I drive myself to the heavily wooded Santa Cruz mountains to a retreat center to see David Whyte, the poet whose work we have listened to throughout the year. Guests sit in the Great Hall as David Whyte reads his poetry and the poetry of other artists. He takes one line and repeats it over and over, letting it sink in. Being in a room with likeminded seekers who value his work is comforting. It is impossible to feel alone. As I sit on the floor in the Saturday afternoon session, my emotions begin to well up with a deep sense of recognition and gratitude. The depth of my connection to myself in that moment is so profound that there is nothing else to do but cry. I can't hold back the tears. I get up, walk out, and begin to weep.

A woman walks up and asks, "May I hug you?" Completely out of character, I say yes to this kind stranger and allow her to hold me as I cry and cry. She does not say a word. She simply holds me until I stop, and then we part. I don't even know her name. I gather myself and go back inside. I can't believe I let down my guard, was completely vulnerable, and allowed a total stranger to care for me. I feel as though I am broken open.

At the end of the weekend, I feel empowered, grounded, and open to the world in new ways. I am going to be okay. I realize being without a man is actually the easy part; learning to be open and vulnerable will be the real test. I think I am ready. I am almost there, almost ready to take the risk.

Gayle

I reach out to Pat, the intuitive who told us about the Blessing Moon. (Before our call, her process is to go into a deep meditation to connect with what she calls Source.) When we're on our call, she begins by saying, "Your family energy is askew; there's an upheaval."

I think to myself, *No shit, Sherlock!*

She suggests "getting into nothingness—spirit is there." That makes sense to me since I do find a calm respite when I meditate.

"You are energetically done with both men," she continues. "It's a blessing in disguise that you will not be with the man you thought you were going to be with. Sometimes we come together, complete a cycle, then we pull apart." A sense of relief and sadness washes over me. She reassures me, "You are going to be okay financially, your husband will be providing something for you, and you have two money streams coming through."

She reminds me of the mantra "I want this or something better," to which I reply in agreement, "Yes, I like to believe something greater this way comes and anything is possible."

"Gayle, you will be married again."

"What?" I spout in disbelief. My heart isn't in the space to comprehend another marriage. I wasn't expecting her to say that.

"You will be married again. It doesn't feel like it's in the blueprint of your incarnation to stay single. Sometimes your cup has to be emptied so it can be filled. Nobody outside of you can guarantee that you'll be in a relationship again. Only you can." And then, like every other therapist has advised me, Pat says, "Right now I want you to have an affair with you."

Oh God, how many times must I hear this? I think.

"You are a fish out of water because your life as you knew

it changed so dramatically." I do my best to absorb her words. "Your greatest gift is self-love. Embrace this time in your life. If your intent is pure, you will manifest it." The session ends with her reiterating that this year for me is about conscious choice and rewriting my narrative to one of liberation and release. "It's an opportunity to reinvent yourself." It's true; I have been reinventing myself. I know who I no longer am, but who will I be when this year is over?

Barb

In April, my company sends about seventy employees to an annual trade show in Las Vegas. My marketing team sets up a big booth for our company's products and services. As usual, Mr. Mister and I head there and stay at the same Hilton Grand Vacations resort. We work like we normally would, but one evening, he stops by my condo. This time I feel like I need to have a conversation with him. I never addressed the issues of our prior affair. He takes a seat on a chair in the living room, and I sit on the couch, a close but comfortable distance from him.

"You know, I changed my life to be with you, and you did nothing," I tell him. There is no angst or frustration in my voice, just clarity. "I gave myself up for you. I stood before you openhearted, and you chose to stay in your miserable life, not escaping the pain."

Surprisingly, he opens up about where he was then and now. He's honest, telling me what was true for him. "I have my integrity now," Mr. Mister says. "I had walked into a room that had no exits. I would need to leave my marriage from a place of integrity." He doesn't make any excuses for struggling with how to have the life he desires. It's clear he is not moving on or moving back. There is something honorable about his confession of how he is stuck. I am not waiting for him. We talk through it all like friends, caring and supportive. That feels good, separate, and whole, even though we are still deeply in love with each other.

"I appreciate your honesty with me," I say, and it's true. His honesty is confirmation that I've freed myself from him in many ways.

But not in all ways.

A few weeks later, we have another conversation. He says his intention is to become single—available. He isn't trying to pretend. I spin out, consumed with his confession of love for me and desire for a future together. The churning, though, doesn't last long. At the beginning of this year, spinning out would have lasted for weeks or months. Within a few days, my feet are back on the ground. I've regained my equilibrium.

Yes, I realize how much I want to have a future with him, but I also realize how that can only be accomplished if I remember who I am and stay on top of my mountain. It hits me again that just because I am in love with him doesn't mean that I am meant to be with him. Alone, apart, or together, I will be okay. The most important question is, how do I have the authentic life I want, which includes my kids, a positive relationship with my ex, and an open, loving relationship with myself?

28

Celebration

Barb

My forty-ninth birthday is coming up, and Gayle and I decide to experiment with our intuition on a road trip to San Francisco. Rather than plan every detail of the weekend, we drive to San Francisco and let the weekend unravel naturally. Our hotel room at the Hilton sits high above the city, and we can see Coit Tower and the entire San Francisco Bay. The weather is perfect. It is one of those gorgeous fogless days that makes us both wonder why we don't live here.

As we drive through the city, we begin playing a game. At every intersection, we ask, "Which way should we turn?" We let our intuition decide. We follow what feels right. We have no maps, no plans. We are not tied to any outcome, just to the experience itself. We spend the day laughing and exploring.

"Oh, look at that little boutique. Let's stop there."

"Let's turn left here."

"This street looks interesting."

We end up in Pacific Heights among the panoramic views of the city and the bay and some of the most expensive homes in the States. We stumble upon a North Beach restaurant with authentic Tuscan cuisine that's been in the city for over fifty years. I remember going into the restaurant with my sister years ago and walking past Herb Caen, a famous journalist who wrote for the *San Francisco Chronicle* for nearly sixty years, dining there. We have cocktails and a bite to eat. Trusting our own autopilot is fun.

Next, we find ourselves in Golden Gate Park. We come across a marker for the 49-Mile Scenic Drive that covers much of San Francisco and are soon surrounded by California poppies. We jump out of the car and take a photo since it is my forty-ninth birthday. We hop back in the car and follow the road to its end, where the famous Cliff House restaurant hugs the rocks at the water's edge. We go inside, order lemon drops, and watch the waves rolling onto the shore of Ocean Beach. The truth is, we are having a fabulous time, and a man is not involved in any way (okay, a man made our drinks, but still)!

Over the next few days, we wander in and out of boutiques and galleries, take in a ballet, eat at world-renowned restaurants, and enjoy cocktails from bars with incredible vistas. We realize, once again, that we make great traveling partners. It is all so easy.

As I turn another year older and the end of this journey is within reach, on most days, I can see myself sitting on top of my own mountain. Those I choose to be with will walk up to meet me here in this place. Truth be told, I still want that to be Mr. Mister, even after all this time. But my world goes on. Meanwhile, I heal and grow and live—openly. I can feel the butterfly of my soul emerging.

29

365 Days

Gayle

Dr. David begins our last session by listening to my story about seeing Mr. Married in the parking lot and hearing that he is going to remain married.

"What was different about that experience?" Dr. David asks.

"It took him saying the truth to me—I'm staying with my wife—to make it crystal clear that a relationship with him is not an option."

"What effect did that have on you?"

"It was a good effect. Now looking back, I can see that, after he asked me out and we began to spend time together, I became attached to him and became the pursuer. I used my Gayle-force to create a web of seduction. I did a lot of the work," I firmly state. "It's clear to me now that I don't want to be his wife."

Dr. David looks up from his notes. "That's quite a difference from a year ago. Do you see how much clarity you have?"

"I deserve so much more than him. I don't look at him the same way now. All of the angst and longing I had for him are gone. It's as if they've been exorcised from my being."

Barb

I recount my recent history with Mr. Mister. I tell Dr. David, "We traveled to Las Vegas, and I was really present with him. We had a long conversation where we put it all on the table. I am moving forward; he is stuck. Freedom comes from what is, and I choose what is. I don't want to go to the hardware store for bread.

"He's lost himself to a toxic relationship. I can't be his therapist. I won't have a relationship with a married man. Nothing has changed except my integrity is back."

"Do you see how this is different from a year ago?" Dr. David asks.

"Well, yeah, there's not an addiction around it now," I say.

In my first session with Dr. David, I'd shared that my life had always had a man in it. Today, in our last session, I see that my life is good. I'm optimistic and I feel happy. I do miss having a romantic lover in my life. That would be the seasoning, though, not the main dish. It's been easy being around Mr. Mister this past month at work. Our relationship is no longer burdened with guilt and shame.

Dr. David says, "I see that you are not seeing the relationship from the lens of regret and bitterness."

"I have this feeling that we will be together someday, but I am not living for it."

I see the potential of dating as play, as a new experience. David reminds me to dip my toe into dating, not jump in. "Now, I'm not up for a guy who is asleep," I tell him. "There's no foregone conclusions; I won't be tied to the outcome. I'm just going to let expectations go and ask myself: Am I having fun in this moment? Am I being open and true to myself?"

Gayle and I are prime examples of going to the places that scare us most. We stood frightened at the edge of a cliff—and we jumped. Freedom and happiness were right there waiting to help us fly. This self-imposed exile has led us to our own power. We took men off the table and then we looked at why they were so important in the first place. Our attachment to men was well overboard. After being with a married man, I had to go back to observe my life and what the hell I was doing. We didn't change the axis of the world; we changed ourselves. Forever.

Dr. David has seen us, created a safe space for us to explore alternative stories, and helped us to rewrite our narrative. Men no longer get to be in the starring role. I am at the center of my story. Gayle is the star of hers.

With the flip of a calendar page, the year is up. We're out of the neutral zone of transition; our new beginning starts now, and it will bring adjustments and challenges of its own. Gayle and I spend the entire day in celebration. First, we have an appointment to see Joan to talk about how we are feeling and our progress. Then we will celebrate with lunch and drinks. Later, we plan to meet up with Hollie and make a night of it.

I pick up Gayle from her house. We are both quiet along the drive we have taken alone to Joan's so many times. The sun is shining on us as we make our way down the winding road and past the pond along the beautifully landscaped lawn. We admire the wisteria and acknowledge the Buddha. Joan is waiting, as she often does, at the door.

"Come in, come in," she says as she greets us with the maternal hugs we have come to expect. She has prepared a ceremony to emphasize our growth, including a booklet of poems that reflect our individual and collective journeys.

As we sit on the couch that has held each of us many times in the last twelve months, we see a large Nautilus on the coffee table. Joan tells us the shell represents the growth from being tightly wound up to unfurling and expanding outward. She then lights a candle and begins by reading the poem "Love after Love" by Derek Walcott for Gayle.

"It will be a feast, Gayle," Joan says, "Your one bright, wild, and precious life. You are loving the 'stranger who was yourself' and being loved in turn by the one who has been with you always!

"What a process you have been through this year—from being willing to stay in a marriage because you didn't want to be alone to becoming a woman who stands tall in her own light, power, and presence. I witness this butterfly moment for you. Know that you have the resources to continue on this journey to love, facing future challenges with the knowledge and wisdom of one who has done her work! Your heart is opening and your compassion is spilling forth. May you grow in love and feast on your life always."

Of course, by now, we are both in tears. Tears of happiness, release, recognition, and gratitude. For me, Joan reads David Whyte's "What to Remember When Waking."

"Oh, my goodness Barbara, so much to remember when waking! I chose this poem because it has a strong message about planning and the importance of committing to wholehearted living. No plans—they're too small anyway. This reminds us to stay open to the 'other world' and to 'your true inheritance.'"

Tears keep sliding down my cheeks as Joan reminds me of the insight that led us to this year, the commitment, and all the work we have done.

"You ladies did the work," Joan says. "But the work is not over."

Dr. David's final letter confirms the truth of Joan's words.

Dear Barb and Gayle,

The end of the year looms closer and closer! Can you believe it? Would your year-ago-June-selves be surprised by where you both are now? What words would they use to describe your growth, your journey, the qualities, and skills you have, and the intentions and goals you envision for yourselves?

Gayle, in terms of your future, you have wanted some assurance that you will not be alone. And yet, in our last meeting, you said:

- *I love being alone.*
- *I don't want a boyfriend.*
- *I see myself as a strong, phenomenal woman.*
- *I'm going with the flow.*
- *I'm not the same person.*
- *I deserve much more; I believe another guy is out there for me.*

From this place of confidence, you went to [an intuitive]. And, of course, to no surprise (like I have said!) she said that you will not be alone—that you will be with an intelligent, easy-on-the-eyes guy who is active and loves the outdoors. Until this man comes into your life, you are moving forward emotionally, spiritually, and psychologically.

Barb, I wish I would have taped our first session when you, in the grip of attachment, said that you could not see yourself without a man; that you had been with a man since you were fifteen-and-a-half years old. Now, you are breaking free of this attachment (and others). You are an observer of yourself. And from this vantage point, you are making healthy decisions.

Here are some quotes from you Barb:
- *I have gone to the places that scare me.*
- *I rescued myself.*
- *I choose freedom.*
- *Life is good; sun is shining.*
- *I'm happy.*
- *The old story is gone.*

You have realized that you need a man who's not asleep and who is working on his own personal growth. From this place of confidence, you are each entertaining the idea of dating. This process will require a new way of relating to men. It will be an experiment. It will be a process of learning not to have expectations. Now you both will put your skills into action in a relational way. Now you will practice connecting with others (including men) from an open, non-attached, present, and mindful place.

Yours sincerely,
David

All the self-help and spiritual work paid off because I finally acted on it in regard to my blind spots. I never would have expected that I'd become a person who allows herself to experience her brokenness. When I stopped resisting and allowed myself to be broken open, I found untouched territory—places within me that I had hidden long ago. Hiding was intended to protect me from pain, but once I faced that pain, I found that it was nothing to be afraid of. Embracing my pain has allowed me to rediscover my gifts, dreams, and desires. I came into the year thinking that Mr. Mister needed to prepare himself for a healthy relationship. Now I realize that this whole year has been about me preparing myself for a relationship with myself first, then, a relationship with another.

My pace has been slow and internally focused. I'm moving into a crawl, which will lead me to walk and eventually run.

Gayle

Today is not just a finish line or accomplishment, but a milestone for the new beginning that lies ahead of us. As we talk about the transformations we've made and what we see as our next unfolding, I never imagined feeling this strong and confident. I am living above the tree line. I am an observer of my thoughts—aware and mindful. The if/then tape no longer plays nonstop in my head. Facing my fear of being alone, I have grown up tremendously. I definitely wear my big girl panties now. If thoughts and desires about Mr. Married still knock on the door of my mind, I will keep the door closed. I recognize them for the illusions they are.

The timing of becoming a therapist is not by accident. The synchronicity of focusing on my inner world has made me more aware, compassionate, and mindful of other people's perceptions. Even my relationship with Barb has been a sort of laboratory for exploring relationship patterns. I've learned that my tendency is to back away and check out emotionally at perceived signs of abandonment. In truth, even though I was committed to Greg, I had emotionally checked out of our marriage chunk by chunk years ago. With Barb, I learned what it is like to truly go deep and experience healthy intimacy with another human being.

Our year without a man may be up, but our friendship with each other is strong. We will still meet on Barb's back deck, eat at our favorite restaurants together, and let each other know if we observe the other falling into old patterns.

We blow out the candle and gather our booklets from Joan. We stand up and hug each other. Joan's nurturing arms send strength into our bodies.

Contentment and clarity join us in the car as we drive back to our quaint town. We pull up to an old brick building on the corner of Commercial and Pine Street and walk into one of our favorite cafés, Mateo's. The sun is shining, and the doors are open. We grab a table at the edge of the open doors and the sidewalk. We feel the sun on our faces, and an immense feeling of freedom washes over us. We order Mateo's famous fish tacos and champagne.

"We did it!" Barb says. "Three hundred sixty-five days without a relationship with a man! It has been an amazing journey, Gayle. I am so glad you said yes and did it with me. I can't imagine doing it without you."

"It has been an honor. I am forever changed. Let's have a toast!" I say, holding up my glass.

"To a year without a man, to all that we have learned, and to all that is possible. To us." We clink glasses.

"To us!"

30

The Years After

Barb

As I was graduating from my year without a man, my daughter, Sammy, was graduating from eighth grade. To celebrate our transitions, we flew to Europe for three weeks. I wanted her to experience Europe and her own power—independence with support. When we landed in France, she immediately figured out the Paris Metro, mapping out where we were and where we were going. I was proud to see her take charge and discover some of her own gifts. Plus it made our travels across the city much easier as I always struggle with directions in a new city.

We started in Paris, staying in a hotel two blocks from the Arc de Triomphe where we happened upon the final stage of the Tour de France. Then we took the train to meet friends in Toulouse at their country home. After that, we flew to Stockholm for four days (the city where Mr. Mister and I started our affair). When we got to our room (at a boutique hotel that Mr. Mister had found several years earlier and had become our home base for work in Sweden), there was a bottle of champagne and a note: "Enjoy the trip, [Mr. Mister]." I appreciated his thoughtfulness, but it didn't trip me up. A few days later, we backtracked to Paris and rented an apartment in the ninth arrondissement for another ten days.

One morning as I was sitting alone at a streetside café, drinking a cappuccino and eating a croissant, a Frenchman came on to me. Even though he spoke little English and I spoke little French, he was intrigued by me and insisted that I spend time with him while in the city. It was a fun conversation, but one that I had no interest in pursuing. No man or romantic hang-up hindered my time with Sammy. I was present and connected with my daughter and myself. And I couldn't have been happier.

Gayle

Three hundred and sixty-five days was not enough to break my addiction. With Barb off to Paris with her daughter and my son graduating from high school and leaving for college, I suddenly felt very alone—and not in the all-one way that Joan had taught me. In fact, I was still holding on to one very big expectation: I thought men would be standing in line waiting to be with the amazing Gayle.

There was nobody. There was certainly no Mr. Married, and my soon-to-be ex-husband was now in a public relationship with the woman who had sent him the text messages all those years ago. She was also the same person I had heard him having sex with during the year.

I was actually alone.

Ironically, the year without a man had become another safety net for me. Without that structure, the weight of loss—my marriage, my home, my emotional affair, my year without a man—overwhelmed me. And I relapsed.

I signed up on match.com right away—and found men who would pay attention to me and want to be with me. For six months, I lost myself in men—some young and hot, some in the middle of divorce, some self-absorbed but "available." I was pretty high on the dopamine rush of it all. The addictive tendencies in me had me going back for more.

Barb saw it happening. "This is not you, Gayle," she told me. It was as if I was on a bender.

Fortunately, I wasn't as alone as I had felt on day 366. I still had my support system (therapist Joan, spiritual teacher and bodyworker Javier, energy worker/intuitive Judith, Barb, and Al-Anon). One day, before another date, I broke down in a session with Joan. She suggested I cancel my plans for the evening.

I can't say no to a guy who wants to go on a date, I thought.

"The choice is actually yours," Joan reminded me.

Is it? Despite all the awareness I had gained during the last year, somehow, I had been oblivious to the fact that I got to choose whether to say yes or no to a man, just like I got to choose who I am and how I will live. So I canceled—even though every cell in my body tried to resist my decision.

That evening I filled the bathtub and slipped into the warm water. I really thought I had passed this life lesson once and for all. *WTF? I feel like a fool. I'm suffering yet again because I want something other than what is.*

The tears started to fall, and I called Barb. She came right over.

"I feel like Jenny on the ledge," I cried, thinking of the movie *Forrest Gump*. "I don't want to be this way anymore."

"Oh, there you are," Barb said gently. She reminded me I

had the paddle I needed to get up this river and back to my own mountain.

That evening, my bender ended. I knew withdrawals might follow, but they would pass eventually. Been there. Done that. Survived.

Barb

I was open to dating, but I knew my boundaries. One of Gayle's boyfriends, Peter, had a friend named Geoff. He was gorgeous, confident, and CEO of his own company. We met on a boat trip on Lake Tahoe and flirted the whole day. I invited him to join me for dinner at my house after a few weeks of flirtatious texting, and we took a sailing trip on San Francisco Bay with Peter and Gayle. Our interactions were flirty and fun, and I was authentic and myself with him from the start.

Come to find out, though, he was separated but still living with his ex-wife and had too many entanglements with her to mention. He told me his plan was to divorce her, but that had been the case for years. Too bad. I was not going down that road again. Even though our mutual attraction was strong, I put an end to our budding relationship. The choice came easily and confirmed that I was in a better place.

Then in the fall, Mr. Mister separated from his wife and moved out of their home. I couldn't believe it. We picked up where we had left off immediately—including the secrecy of our relationship. After all, he was recently separated, and we still worked in the same company and with the same judgmental people. After a while, though, the secrecy started to eat at me. I had just spent a year working through a lot of shit so that I could be more authentic and open. So why was I back in this place, down at the bottom of my mountain meeting Mr. Mister where he was rather than him coming up to meet me?

He agreed to see Joan with me. "I love you and want to be with you, but I'm done," I told him. "I'm not gonna live a secret life. If you want to do that, it's fine, but it won't be with me."

"How does that make you feel?" Joan asked Mr. Mister.

"I want her to do what she needs to do to be happy," he replied, but as he said those words, he reached out and grabbed my arm. Joan pointed out the disconnection between his real feelings reflected in his body language and his words—it couldn't have been more apparent.

I hoped his answer would have been different, but it wasn't. I had to accept what is. I could not change him. I could not compromise my relationship with myself or the desire to have deep and meaningful relationships out in the open. My choice was clear. I had to leave Mr. Mister behind.

One day at work, I received a bouquet of flowers that Gayle's boyfriend, Peter, had sent to her. They were a big, beautiful mix of white roses and green foliage and were sent to my office to make delivery easier for the florist. Mr. Mister walked by my office, stopped, came in, and with a surprised look on his face, asked me where the flowers came from. I said something about them coming from a friend but didn't give up any additional details. After all, that was none of his business. From the look on his face, I could tell he worried that they were from a suitor. It gave me a little pleasure to know that he was suffering too.

Gayle

I finally got the whirlwind romance I was looking for. Peter was a dream. When we met, we kissed before we ever said hello. Our first date was at Squaw Valley Resort and was twelve hours of nonstop talking. For a few months, we rushed forward. He took me to Napa Valley, planned outings in Tahoe, scheduled couples' massages, left rose petals on the floor of hotel rooms. I felt like I was in an episode of *The Bachelorette*. Madly in love, I could see our future together. I ignored the facts that he lived too far away, his kids and mine would not have gotten along, and he wasn't in a position to make me a priority. The speed and over-the-top romance overshadowed the question of whether we would be good partners with similar values. The truth was that I was in love with the idea of this man in the suit rather than the man himself.

Nine months later he broke my heart.

Our breakup cracked open the grief that was still deep inside me from Greg and Mr. Married. Deep sadness poured out of me, and in that pain, I decided to guard my heart. I shifted my mental and emotional energy back to my therapy licensure, setting up my own practice, and authentically living as a confident, independent woman. I was still dependent on Greg's financial support, but I needed and wanted to move on.

My mind knew happiness wouldn't come from a man (and reality had proven that); my heart had been slow in catching on. I knew that eventually I'd be in another relationship, but I had no clue how to date in a healthy way. At forty-nine, online dating was all new to me, and I had gone into it with no rulebook or boundaries. My dating history included only my high school boyfriend/fiancé, Chris, and Greg. What I'd done with

Mr. Married certainly didn't count as "dating."

Barb and I had created a strategy for our year of being man-free, but now I had to create a strategy for being with a man. The choices were mine.

When I organically met Dino, nine years my junior, he felt safe. He was a bartender who didn't drink and had no cellphone, no ambitions of marriage, and very little money. There was no chance he would ever want to marry me. As a man of integrity, he was honest about himself from the get-go. We hit it off and dated for a few years. Our relationship was real, authentic, and healthier than any other romance. I was guarded, but I stayed on top of my mountain and was able to be with Dino without turning it into an obsession or basing my happiness on the outcome.

Ultimately, Dino told me I deserved to be in a committed relationship with someone who would travel with me, enjoy the same nice things I enjoyed, and wanted a long-term partnership. "You know I can't give that to you," he said in kindness. He was right. I knew what he saw about me was true. We parted ways; my heart stayed strong. We remain friends and are close even today. Dino was my first relationship in a new dating direction.

Not long after Dino, I found a one-year program called Dating With Dignity from the Institute for Living Courageously. It educated me about how to date with confidence based on values and in control of my decisions. This was exactly what helped me stay away from my obsessive relational tendencies. I finally had a playbook and five non-negotiable criteria: health (physically, mentally, environmentally), financial security and responsibility, fun/adventurous, integrity, and presence (confident and self-aware). And I used it.

Slowly, I accepted dates with two goals in mind: 1) to be present and have fun, and 2) to collect data to see if a man met *my* criteria for a partner. I finally had the support and framework to choose wisely and intentionally—who to date, who to say no to, when to exit, when to dive in, and even what to do if/when someone broke my heart. More and more, I found that I was choosing myself first over a man and the idea of the "perfect" relationship.

I still want that feeling of love with a man who can hold me and walk side by side with me, but I love my freedom and space—being able to go to bed at any time I want, leaving the window cracked even if it's snowing outside, watching what I want on TV, and having breakfast for dinner if I feel like it. I am no longer running if/then scenarios in my mind.

On top of my own mountain is a guilt-free, drug-free, drama-free zone. Like the minimum height requirement at a carnival ride, my sign at tree line reads, "Must have a high level of integrity to enter." Up here is where I find serenity and the freedom of being all-one with myself.

31

—

EPILOGUE

And the day came when the risk to remain tight in a bud
was more painful than the risk it took to blossom.

—Anaïs Nin

Gayle finalized her divorce. She and Greg rarely spoke after that. Sadly, Greg died the week the world shut down due to COVID-19.

Mr. Married stayed married.

Today, Gayle is a licensed psychotherapist and runs The Empowerment Center, where she provides psychotherapy, coaching, and mediation services, helping women conquer their fears of being alone and empowering them to stand confidently on their own two feet.

Gayle is happily single and still lives in her "divorce house." She knows she will eventually have a healthy romantic relationship on her own terms, but for now she is perfectly content living on her own in Nevada City, California, traveling solo and with girlfriends, and running a thriving private practice.

Gayle is also a breast cancer survivor. A few years after the year without a man, Gayle was diagnosed with breast cancer and underwent a double mastectomy and reconstructive surgery. It threatened another one of her long-held identities: a woman who could lead with her sexuality and physical appearance. She heard the message loudly and clearly from the universe: *Your body doesn't define who you are.* From the biopsy appointment and through eleven surgeries, Barb was by Gayle's side. Today, Gayle is cancer-free and passionate about a lifestyle that includes healthy food, low stress, yoga, meditation, and following what feels light.

Barb and Steve, though divorced, remain friends and active co-parents.

In a twist no one could have foreseen, Mr. Mister actually showed up on Barb's doorstep, professed his love, and committed to creating a healthy open life with her.

As Barb was cleaning out her car a couple of weeks after their session with Joan, she found Mr. Mister's baseball cap under the passenger's seat. He had left it in her car after they had done a friendly bike ride in Lake Tahoe. She called to let him know that she had his hat. He told her that he was on his way right then to their CEO's house to tell him that he wanted to be with Barb. Mr. Mister came to her house immediately after. As Barb stood in her kitchen with her hand on her hip as if to say, *I'll believe it when I see it*, Mr. Mister proceeded to tell her, "I love you. I want you to wake up every day knowing that I adore you, appreciate you, that I am your biggest fan. I want you to know how much I love you and that I chose you."

Eventually, Barb made the decision to walk away from her successful career and took a year off work altogether.

After more than a decade together, Barb and Mr. Mister were married on their beautiful yacht and lived a life of true partnership. Barb, whose independence had always kept her from experiencing love and connection at the deepest levels, created that in her relationship with Mr. Mister. She did, as the old woman told her in her past life regression, let him love her.

On March 27, 2023, Mr. Mister brought breakfast to Barb in her home office and went out for his morning run, where he died of a massive heart attack. Barb is taking the lessons learned in the year without a man with her as she travels this new, unknown path.

Gayle and Barb still have their vision boards from 2011. They remain each other's "person" and can still be found on Barb's back deck supporting each other's spiritual growth and contemplating life and all its mysteries.

References

Brown, Brené. *The Power of Vulnerability: Teachings of Authenticity, Connection, and Courage.* Louisville, CO: Sounds True, 2010.

Chödrön, Pema. *When Things Fall Apart: Heart Advice for Difficult Times.* Boulder, CO: Shambhala Publications, 1996.

Psychotherapy Networker. "David White – The Journey." YouTube video, 3:03. April 9, 2009. youtube.com/watch?v=6PK3GhnHOJc&ab_channel=Psychotherapy-Networker.

Rubin, Lawrence. "David Nylund on Narrative Therapy, Curiosity and Queertopia." psychotherapy.net. 2019. psychotherapy.net/interview/nylund-interview.

William Bridges Associates. "Bridges Transition Model." Accessed December 1, 2023. wmbridges.com/about/what-is-transition.

Winfrey, Oprah. "Jane Fonda on Perfection." *Oprah's Master Class*, Season 2, Episode 201. January 8, 2012. oprah.com/own-master-class/jane-fonda-on-perfection-video.

Resources

Many resources helped us throughout the Year Without a Man. These are a few of our favorites. For a comprehensive list of resources, visit www.ayearwithoutaman.com.

Books

Committed: A Skeptic Makes Peace with Marriage by Elizabeth Gilbert

Eat, Pray, Love: One Woman's Search for Everything Across Italy, India, and Indonesia by Elizabeth Gilbert

The Four Agreements: A Practical Guide to Personal Freedom by Don Miguel Ruiz

The Gifts of Imperfection by Brené Brown

If the Buddha Dated: A Handbook for Finding Love on a Spiritual Path by Charlotte Kasl

Managing Transitions: Making the Most of Change by William Bridges with Susan Bridges

The Artist's Way at Work: Riding the Dragon by Mark Bryan, Julia Cameron, and Catherine A. Allen

Not "Just Friends": Rebuilding Trust and Recovering Your Sanity After Infidelity by Shirley P. Glass with Jean Coppock Staeheli

The Power of Now: A Guide to Spiritual Enlightenment by
    Eckhart Tolle

When Things Fall Apart: Heart Advice for Difficult Times by
    Pema Chödrön

Other

Brown, Brené. "The Power of Vulnerability."
    TED Talk. June 2010. ted.com/talks/
    brene_brown_the_power_of_vulnerability?language=en.

Dating With Dignity through the Institute for Living
    Courageously. datingwithdignity.com/about.

The Poetry of Self-Compassion audio CD by David Whyte.

Acknowledgments

Heartfelt thanks to everyone who helped us on the journey of the Year Without a Man and to the creation of this book. It has always been important for us to share our story in the hopes that others will be inspired to find freedom from suffering. Thank you, Dr. Jayanath Abeywickrama, Joan Goddard, MFT, Itamar Vinitzky, PhD, NMT, Hollie Grimaldi-Flores, Katie Rubin, Andrea Vinley Converse, and KN Literary Arts. We are also eternally grateful for each other.

The depth of transformation that we experienced during the year would not have been as significant without the guidance of Dr. David Nylund and his instrumental work with Narrative Therapy.

Barb would like to extend a special thank you to her wonderful children, Brent, Nicole, and Sammy, and to her five grandchildren, Callel, Ciauss, Warren, Lexi, and Chloe, for their unconditional love and support; to her sister, Debbie, for always being by her side; and to her husband, Shawn, for teaching her about deep and abiding love.

Gayle wholeheartedly extends gratitude and love to her children, Sierra, Carley, and Cody; to her mom; and to her posse of close friends: Teri Dougherty, Mimi Simmons, Holly Hermansen, Asha Caravelli, and Mike Hallroan, who were on the receiving end of countless tearful phone calls, providing loving support and reassurance throughout her Year Without a Man.

Discover the power of community. Join our vibrant safe haven of support and connection. Explore beyond the book at www.ayearwithoutaman.com and be part of something extraordinary!

Barb & Gayle

Cliff House 2011

About the Authors

Barbara DeHart's early love of technology led to a career in media and entertainment tech where she has developed global teams to move products from the idea stage, through development, and out to the market. Committed to developing tomorrow's female leaders, she has mentored many female executives, coached women-led technology companies with nonprofit FourthWave Accelerator, and co-founded Indivisible Women of Nevada County, a grass roots organization supporting women to become engaged in civic and political leadership.

Deeply motivated to a life of authenticity, Barbara has taken two yearlong timeouts to dive more deeply into her relationships and her career. She often speaks at women's events and facilitates workshops on women's empowerment, organizational and personal transitions, and creativity. Barb has raised two children who are happy, healthy adults. She shares five grandchildren with her soulmate and husband, Shawn (aka Poppy), with whom she spent more than a decade, living their dream life together until his premature death in 2023.

Barbara's life was interrupted by a medical crisis that led to a yearlong timeout to better understand her relationship with men and herself. A year without a man helped her recognize and heal the wounds of her early life and become a woman able to engage in healthy romantic relationships.

Gayle Long is a licensed marriage and family therapist and runs The Empowerment Center, where she provides psychotherapy, coaching, and mediation services. Her specialty is working as a women's divorce transition coach, helping women conquer their fears of being alone and empowering them to stand confidently on their own two feet. She counsels people on how to shift devastating relationship loss into positive growth. Her greatest joy is helping clients and witnessing their personal growth and transformation. She is also the former president of the Conflict Resolution Center of Nevada County. Gayle holds two master's degrees: one in clinical psychology and another in counseling psychology. She is also a speaker and leads personal empowerment and compassionate communication workshops.

The year without a man (and the years after) launched Gayle into the second half of life as a newly independent woman. She enjoys living on her own in Nevada City, California. All three of her children are grown and married, and she is now a proud "glammy." A breast cancer survivor, Gayle is passionate about a healthy lifestyle that includes clean food and low stress. She loves being in nature, walking the local trails, traveling near and far with friends, pursuing personal growth, creative cooking, and spending time with her children.